HOW TO HELP SOMEONE WITH ANXIETY

WELBECK
BALANCE

ABOUT THE AUTHOR

Rachel M Allan is a counselling psychologist who specializes in sharing psychological knowledge in an accessible way. She combines her role in an adult NHS mental health service with running a successful private psychology practice. She is a sought-after speaker, trainer and commentator in the field of mental health and wellbeing. Rachel lives with her husband, two children, and beloved cat in Glasgow, Scotland.

A Trigger Book
Published by Welbeck Balance
An imprint of Welbeck Publishing Group
20 Mortimer Street
London W1T 3JW

First published by Welbeck Balance in 2021

A CIP catalogue record for this book is available from the British Library

ISBN
Trade Paperback – 9781789562668

Typeset by Lapiz Digital Services
Printed in Dubai

10 9 8 7 6 5 4 3 2 1

Note/Disclaimer

Welbeck Balance encourages diversity and different viewpoints. However, all views,
thoughts, and opinions expressed in this book are the author's own and are not
necessarily representative of Welbeck Publishing Group as an organization. All
material in this book is set out in good faith for general guidance; no liability can
be accepted for loss or expense incurred in following the information given. In
particular, this book is not intended to replace expert medical or psychiatric advice.
It is intended for informational purposes only and for your own personal use and
guidance. It is not intended to diagnose, treat or act as a substitute for professional
medical advice. Professional advice should be sought if desired before embarking
on any health-related programme.

www.welbeckpublishing.com

To my parents, Finlay and Norma MacLeod.

CONTENTS

Introduction   xi

1 So, What is Anxiety?   1
2 A Different Kind of Conversation   21
3 Learning the Art of Listening   31
4 Forming an Understanding   52
5 Putting Anxiety in Context   77
6 Reframing Anxious Thoughts   98
7 The Role of Behaviour   115
8 Practical Approaches   147
9 Bringing it All Together   169
10 When to Seek Professional Help   180
11 Your Role in Recovery   192

Final Thoughts   210

Acknowledgements   212
Endnotes   214
Useful Resources   216

INTRODUCTION

In recent years, conversations about mental health have become more public and more frequent. Awareness campaigns, official guidelines and common sense all make the same plea to those who are suffering: 'Talk to someone. Reach out. Ask for help. Tell someone how you feel.'

What if that someone is you? What if it is *your* friend, relative or partner who is struggling and suffering, and you are looking on helplessly, not knowing how best to support them?

In my work as a therapist, I see how important a good support system can be for someone who is living with anxiety. None of us lives in a bubble; our difficulties play out in our roles, relationships and social networks. Equally, having good support around us can be a key factor in helping us make a lasting change.

When we see someone we care for suffering, our instinct is to do what we can to ease their situation, but sometimes, with the best will in the world, our actions can end up feeding the problem.

The aim of this book is to give you the information and guidance you need to support someone who you know is mind when social anxiety thoughts threaten to take hold. I no longer allow it to limit my decisions, relationships or ambitions. Its voice remains with me, but it is quieter and better managed. So those who meet me would probably never know.

THE APPROACHES USED IN THIS BOOK

In my role as a therapist, I see clients experiencing all kinds of difficulties, but there is almost always an element of anxiety in the picture. I have come to recognize that while each person's situation is different, there are key approaches that tend to lead to the biggest breakthroughs with anxiety.

There are many psychological therapies and they all address anxiety slightly differently. In this book, the approaches I share with you are based largely on Cognitive Behavioural Therapy, or CBT. Research evidence demonstrates that CBT is an effective way of tackling anxiety,[i] and I regularly see first-hand how empowering CBT-based strategies and techniques can be for those seeking to live better with anxiety.

CBT has expanded and evolved over recent years, and it now incorporates ideas from other therapies. These include approaches such as Mindfulness and Acceptance and Commitment Therapy (ACT), which have been proven to be effective for treating anxiety.[ii]

The ideas I will share with you in this book are based on these evidence-based therapeutic approaches, and on my experience of what has worked best for my clients in clinical practice.

HOW THIS BOOK WORKS

This book is not a one-size-fits-all approach to responding to distress, nor is it a treatment manual for anxiety. Its aim is to explore how you can help someone struggling with anxiety make sense of their experience, and how that can form a basis for helping them to make some changes.

> "The focus of this book is not to *sort out*, or to *fix*, but to help you act as an ally, in a way that may help someone move forward and to live better with anxiety."

Right from the beginning, it is important to be clear about what I hope will be our shared endeavour on this journey together. I hope you will join me in seeking to find ways to be genuinely helpful and empowering to the person you hope to support. The focus is not to *sort out*, or to *fix*, but to help you act as an ally and comrade, in a way that may help your loved one move forward and to live better with anxiety.

THE TURN FRAMEWORK

Throughout the book, a simple framework called TURN is used as a reference point for helping someone with anxiety. TURN stands for:

- **T**ime
- **U**nderstanding
- **R**eframing and Redirecting
- **N**ew Approach

ANXIETY STORIES

The book follows the stories of three individuals whose lives are being adversely affected by anxiety. These examples are used to explore the ways in which anxiety can manifest, and to illustrate how someone's support can make a difference. These stories are not based on any one individual. Each one of them represents some of the common patterns I see in relation to anxiety.

Some aspects of these scenarios might resonate with elements of your own experience of trying to support someone struggling with anxiety. We will follow these characters, and the role of their supporters in their anxiety journey, as we move through each stage of the book.

INTRODUCTION

Catriona is in her final year studying law at university. Increasingly, she has been finding it difficult to sit exams, to the point that she is considering dropping out. As the final exam period approaches, she has been feeling increasingly panicky and overwhelmed. She has been lying awake at night, with her mind racing about what might come up in the exams. She is becoming increasingly tearful and panicky when she visits the library or sits down to revise. Robert and Angela, Catriona's parents, want to find ways to help her so that what's happening doesn't impact her future.

Despite having received top grades throughout her studies, Catriona fears that it could all come crashing down at any point. Her parents constantly remind her how well she has done up until now, and reassure her that she has nothing to worry about. Every time Catriona submits a piece of work or is going to sit an exam, she anticipates that this will be the time she fails. She puts pressure on herself to study every moment she can. She analyzes every piece of feedback she receives and focuses on any negative comments.

Recently, Catriona had the opportunity to apply for an exciting internship, but missed the deadline for the application because she was convinced what she had written would not be good enough and that she would embarrass herself by applying.

In many areas of our life, anxiety serves as a useful indicator that we need to act. Every day, our anxiety serves the function of keeping us safe, alive and accountable.

"I do not talk about *having* anxiety; I talk about *living with* anxiety. That is because we all *have* anxiety and it is essential to our survival."

THE ANXIETY SCALE

We all experience anxiety at different levels. The extent to which anxiety shows up for us can ebb and flow depending on what is going on in our lives. We might see ourselves as someone who has a naturally anxious temperament. I hear this in my clinical work sometimes, when a client might describe themselves as 'an anxious person'. Early life experiences and relationships can affect how prone we are to anxiety. For example, growing up with a highly anxious parent, or in an environment with a high level of uncertainty might make us more prone to anxiety. Other times, anxiety can show up all of a sudden, often related to a loss, trauma or transition.

Anxiety exists on a continuum, and the experience is constantly in motion. You may have noticed that I do not talk about *having* anxiety; I talk about *living with* anxiety. That is because we all *have* anxiety and, as we have discovered, it is essential to our survival.

The higher we move up the anxiety scale, the more problematic the anxiety tends to become. The experience ranges from being something that keeps us safe to being something that is distressing and limiting.

You can probably think of ways in which anxiety shows up in the life of the person you are seeking to help. You may have witnessed the distress and darkness that can form part of the experience of severe anxiety.

My aim is to empower you to support someone going through this experience to live better with anxiety. Living well with anxiety doesn't come from getting rid of every anxious thought and feeling; it comes from the relationship we have with anxiety. We cannot control anxiety itself. What we can control is how we respond to it and make sense of it, and how we carry it with us as we go through our lives.

I hope, from this position, you will feel empowered to support someone with anxiety to thrive.

WHAT DOES ANXIETY FEEL LIKE?

We tend to think of anxiety as a description of a mental experience, but usually the most distinctive signs come from our bodies. The churning stomach, the heart racing, the face going red, the sweaty palms, the stuttering speech. It might involve feeling stuck to the spot, paralyzed, sick or as if we can't breathe. It can make us sweat, or feel faint, warm or like we are having a heart attack. Call it dread, panic, fear, terror or anxiety; we all know the feeling.

When I ask my clients to tell me how anxiety feels for them, I hear things like:

- 'A sinking feeling in the pit of my stomach.'
- 'Like I can't catch my breath.'
- 'A big knot in my chest that gets tighter and tighter.'
- 'Blind panic.'
- 'My mind racing at 100 miles an hour.'
- 'Worrying more and more until my thoughts feel out of control.'
- 'The constant feeling that something awful is about to happen.'
- 'Never being able to relax.'
- 'Imagining the worst possible outcome and being terrified that it will come true.'
- 'The feeling of being in a nightmare and not being able to wake up.'

Reading the above may have made you recall times in your own life when you have felt the overwhelming sensation of anxiety.

It might have been when you faced being evaluated, perhaps when going into a meeting or taking your driving test. Or maybe it is the feeling you get when, during an uncertain time, your mind spirals into imagining a worst-case scenario.

STARTING WITH OURSELVES

When we are trying to find ways of helping someone who is struggling, one of the most helpful things we can do is reflect on our own lives and experiences.

Of course, none of us share exactly the same experience. But tuning in to how anxiety has shown up in our own lives can help us get closer to understanding what it might be like for others.

"Being in touch with our own experience of anxiety can be a useful starting point as we prepare to reach out to help someone else."

Later in the book, we will explore whether sharing your own experiences or struggles with anxiety can ever be helpful when supporting someone with anxiety. For now, I am inviting you to spend a moment in reflection. Being in touch with our own experience of anxiety (whether we decide to share that or not) can be a useful starting point as we prepare to reach out to help someone else.

So, before we delve in to learning more about anxiety, I would like you to take a moment to connect with your own experience of anxiety.

HOW TO HELP

Think of a time in your own life when you felt scared, nervous, anxious or overwhelmed. It might be useful to write down your reflections in a notebook or journal.

- What can you remember about that experience?
- What was going on in your mind?
- How did you feel in your body?
- What did you do to cope?
- What was the outcome?
- Did you learn anything about dealing with anxiety from that experience?

THE *WHOOSH*

First and foremost, anxiety is a physical experience. If you were sleeping at home in the middle of the night and you were woken by a loud crash, how would you feel? Chances are you would experience an automatic physical response and quickly sit up with your eyes wide open.

6

That physical response would happen instantly – *whoosh*. It would not usually involve taking the time to make a considered assessment and concluding, 'I could be in danger here, I better act.' The response would be automatic.

When we face immediate threat, we do not have time to carry out a balanced and considered risk assessment. That is not how our mind works when we are in danger. In order to keep ourselves safe, we are primed to have an instant physical response, preparing us to act instantly. *Whoosh*.

That is the great thing about how our physiological system works. It is designed to keep us safe. And part of how it does that is by responding quickly and decisively when faced with a threat. Our top priority is survival, and we are equipped accordingly. We have a whole system dedicated to alerting us to threat, and setting off functions in the body with the purpose of keeping us safe.

You have probably heard of this survival-based response being called the fight-or-flight response.

THE SMOKE DETECTOR

The role of our fight-or-flight response is to keep us safe. It is part of a system that works a bit like a smoke detector. Its job is to activate when threat is detected at a certain threshold. Like a smoke detector, the threat system sits in waiting. It is programmed to activate in response to certain cues in the environment that may indicate risk of harm or a threat to safety.

When something enters our environment that could be a threat to our safety or our physical integrity, the threat system activates, setting off a series of physiological events in the body. This is the activation of what is commonly known as the fight-or-flight response. It is the *whoosh* of physical responses, which occurs when we detect a threat.

It is *not* the job of the threat system to analyze the information in our environment and reach a considered conclusion about the seriousness of it; its job is to detect the presence of threat and initiate a physiological response.

Just like the job of a smoke detector is not to work out whether smoke in the environment indicates an engulfing fire or a burnt piece of toast, the smoke detector's job is simply to activate if a certain level smoke is detected in the air.

HOW TO HELP

- Remember that the ultimate function of anxiety is to keep us safe.
- Be aware that struggling with anxiety does not mean someone is broken or needs to be fixed; it may just mean that their inner safety system is at the more sensitive end of the scale.
- Ask the person experiencing anxiety to share with you what anxiety feels like in their body. What happens for them when the smoke detector activates and they get the *whoosh*?

SHOULD WE CATEGORIZE ANXIETY?

The various ways anxiety can show up are sometimes divided into categories based on common patterns (see page 10), but these may not necessarily capture every pattern that anxiety can follow. Sometimes the experience may span more than one category, fit with different categories at different times or fit with none.

We can probably all recognize ourselves in some of the different anxiety patterns and we might be aware of certain circumstances and certain types of stress that make us more likely to feel these at different times.

A medical approach tends to understand distressing anxiety patterns in the same way as physical illnesses, making sense of the emotions and behaviours that make up the experience of anxiety as *symptoms*. There are different categories or disorders defined by different collections of symptoms. Mental health professionals who work in this way will refer to a diagnostic manual that classifies different disorders. For some people, this is a useful framework for making sense of difficult mental experiences, including different types of anxiety. A person experiencing anxiety may have a diagnosis of a particular anxiety disorder, or they may have an idea about which disorder – if any – they might identify with.

The DSM-5 (*Diagnostic and Statistical Manual for Mental Disorders*)[iii] is a diagnostic manual published by the American

Psychiatric Association. It is a widely used point of reference for classifying patterns of mental experience, using standard criteria.

Professionals such as psychiatrists, psychologists, and others might refer to the DSM-5, or other similar manuals, to categorize or diagnose different types of mental distress.

COMMON PATTERNS OF ANXIETY

You might recognize some of the following classifications and descriptions, which are based on the classification of anxiety in DSM-5:

OCD: For some people, unwanted and distressing thoughts and feelings, which occur persistently, are tied up with a strong urge to carry out certain rituals or behaviours. This pattern is sometimes identified as obsessional-compulsive disorder, or OCD.

Social anxiety: For some, anxious thoughts and feelings relate to how we come across to others, and fearing that we will be judged negatively. These fears may relate to specific social contexts and can lead to avoidance of those contexts. This type of pattern is sometimes identified as social anxiety or social phobia.

Post-traumatic stress disorder (PTSD): Anxiety can sometimes be the result of having experienced a distressing event where we have faced harm, being overpowered, or not being in control. This can be one specific event or a prolonged experience over time. We may feel like we are reliving what happened in the present and going through the distress over and over again. It can make us feel jumpy and panicky, and cause us to avoid things that remind us of that experience.

Panic disorder: Sometimes a physical experience or symptoms like a pain or a change in breathing can make us so anxious that we believe we are out of control or about to die. This can be an intense surge of anxiety in the body, sometimes known as a panic attack. Panic attacks may lead to avoiding situations or triggers that may set off scary physical experiences. Frequent and debilitating panic attacks are sometimes identified as panic disorder.

Generalized anxiety disorder: Sometimes, rather than being focused on one particular situation or fear, anxiety is a general sense of dread and doom that something bad is going to happen, and that when it does we will not be able to cope with it. Those who experience this kind of anxiety might be troubled by overthinking, constant worrying about the future and feelings of distress about the unknown.

You may notice that each of these patterns have something in common: they begin with a surge of fear or distress, followed by a strategy to try to bring that distress down.

An important thing to notice is that the pattern does not simply end with the use of coping strategies. Often, the coping strategies – be it checking, avoiding, worrying or something else – can feed back in to the anxious thoughts and feelings.

This is an important feature of anxiety patterns, and something we will look at in more detail later on.

WHAT NAME SHOULD WE GIVE IT?

For some people, having a clear name or diagnostic term to describe their experience can be helpful and empowering. Receiving a diagnosis for a specific anxiety disorder can feel like a relief, and represent a positive step toward accessing help. It can also be an important way of feeling that the experience of anxiety, and the distress that goes with it, is seen, acknowledged and validated.

"Each person's experience of anxiety, and relationship with it, is in the unique context of their own experience and their own lives."

Categorizing anxiety can also be a useful way of describing a pattern of anxiety without having to go into detail about *our* specific experience of it. It can help articulate the struggles of anxiety in abbreviated terms. It can also be an important way to connect with services and other help available.

For others, the use of such terminology can feel unhelpful and disempowering, particularly describing the experience of anxiety as a 'disorder'. Each person's experience of anxiety, and relationship with it, is in the unique context of their own experience and their own lives. For some people, it can feel like a diagnostic label oversimplifies the varied and complex nature of anxiety. To label our most complex, painful and difficult patterns using one term can feel reductive.

When anxiety shows up in our lives, it usually occurs in a complex and unique set of circumstances. There may be things from the past that have made us more prone to anxiety. There may be stressful events or pressures in the present that have made us more vulnerable.

At any given time, our experience is made up of the interweaving of our past experiences, our present circumstances and our learned ways of coping with what life gives us. For some, having a label to capture the essence of that experience can be important and empowering; for others it can create an unhelpful barrier, and add to existing problems.

STIGMA

Despite the growing awareness around mental health, there can still be shame and stigma attached to having a mental health problem, or diagnosed condition.

Using diagnostic terms to describe or define anxiety can risk making the person experiencing anxiety somehow different to those who do not struggle with anxiety. This in itself can be problematic because when someone is identified as different, it can put that person at a distance from others. It may open them up to discrimination or being seen in the context of unhelpful stereotypes associated with certain anxiety disorders.

"The antidote to stigma is embracing shared humanity. The antidote to distance is connection. Being willing to talk about anxiety is your biggest asset."

The experience of feeling different or separate from others can influence how we see ourselves. If we are held at a distance, or experience stigma repeatedly, we can feel powerless. That powerlessness can lead to a sense of hopelessness that not only are we different, but we are not able to do anything to change our situation. If that happens, it can be harder to access hope and to connect with the things that can improve our situation.

The antidote to stigma is embracing shared humanity. The antidote to distance is connection. And in the context of helping someone with anxiety, being willing to talk about anxiety is your biggest asset. If you can normalize talking about emotions, mental health, stresses and fears with the person you want to support, you will set a powerful foundation for helping them with anxiety.

We will explore this subject much further later in the book. But from the very beginning of our journey of supporting you to help someone experiencing anxiety, I want to encourage you to talk openly about mental health.

FINDING A SHARED LANGUAGE

In order to be in a position to help, it is important to think about how our language and terminology can reveal our attitude toward helping someone close to us who is struggling, or in distress. Ultimately, the important thing is that the way we understand and talk about their difficulties reflects what makes sense to *them*.

You may have ideas about whether the experience of the person you want to support fits with a certain pattern (see page 10). That person may even have received a diagnosis of a particular anxiety disorder. But before you take on the language of diagnosis and illness, check with the person that it makes sense to them. Does it make them feel better understood and supported? Or does it cause them to feel in any way powerless, stuck or hopeless?

When I work with clients who are struggling with anxiety, I often ask them how they would like us to refer to their experience. Some people prefer using the diagnostic term (e.g. 'my OCD'). Others like to choose their own description or terminology (e.g. 'the fear').

The most important thing is not the terminology; it is that you find a shared language with the person you are supporting that reflects how they make sense of their own experience.

Finding the most empowering language to talk about distress is a great start to helping the person who is struggling open up to change. From that basis, you can work together to create opportunities for empowerment over anxiety.

HOW TO HELP

- Normalize talking about mental health with the person you are supporting.
- Invite a conversation with them about how they would like to refer to their experience of anxiety.
- If they have received a diagnosis, ask them if the diagnosis is meaningful for them.
- Try to establish whether using a diagnostic term has an empowering or a disempowering effect. The easiest way to do this is to ask.
- Endeavour to use your loved one's preferred terminology when referring to their experience of anxiety.

LIVING WELL WITH ANXIETY

When I start work with clients, I always ask the same questions during an initial conversation. They go something like this:

'If this were to go really well, and things improved a great deal for you, what would that look like?'

'If you were able to manage anxiety a whole lot better, what kind of things would you be able to do that you can't do right now?'

At this stage in the conversation, the person you are supporting might say that all they want is to get rid of anxiety. You might have noticed that I don't ever talk about 'getting rid' of anxiety. Instead I talk about managing anxiety, or living better with anxiety. Here's why:

If we seek to get rid of something, we are setting ourselves up in opposition to that thing. As we have seen already, the experience of anxiety is an important part of being human. If we set ourselves up to try to get rid of that, then:

1. We could be setting ourselves up to fail.
2. We are setting up a battle or struggle, with a winner or a loser.

Surely it makes more sense to aim to live harmoniously with anxiety? We can implement ways of managing anxiety and reducing the extent to which it limits our lives. But we can do this from a position of recognizing anxiety as an important part of us, rather than taking an oppositional stance and seeking to eliminate the experience altogether.

Anyone living with a high level of anxiety has probably already tried ways of attempting to control that anxiety.

As you read the anxiety stories, you will see that Mishka stays at home because it is too anxiety-provoking to go out, and George constantly checks on his family because the reassurance gives him temporary relief.

It is natural to try to gain control over difficult experiences. I am sure we have all, at one point or another, worried, over-analyzed or avoided situations that make us anxious because that gave us a sense of having some control. These approaches to 'getting rid' of anxiety usually lead to two outcomes.

First, you end up spending so much time and energy trying to get rid of anxiety that you end up locked in a pattern that is even more restrictive and distressing than the original anxiety. Secondly, you end up missing out on the parts of life that you enjoy and that matter to you because you have been so focused on trying to get rid of anxiety.

Look at Catriona, missing out on the opportunity of a brilliant internship because she avoided the anxiety that would go with putting herself forward.

Our attempts to control anxiety can limit our lives in all kinds of ways.

It is therefore a good idea to try to move the conversation beyond 'How do I get rid of anxiety?' Perhaps you can reflect with the person you are supporting on what they would like to do, or to achieve, if they were able to live better with anxiety.

It is important to spend some time helping the other person think about what they actually want their life to look like. And to do that, they need to get clear on what a rich and meaningful life could look like for them, if they were able to live well with anxiety.

SUMMARY

- Anxiety is part of human experience, and its primary purpose is to keep us safe.
- The physical signs of anxiety are part of what is known as the fight-or-flight response. This is a collection of physical changes that typically go with feeling anxious.
- Anxiety becomes problematic when it keeps us in a distressed state for extended periods of time, and gets in the way of us living our life in the way that we want.
- There is no right or wrong way to describe anxiety. The important thing is that the person you are supporting is comfortable with the language you use to talk about it.

- Trying to control or get rid of anxiety can cause us to get stuck in a restrictive pattern of behaviour.
- An alternative to trying to *escape* anxiety is to move toward *living better with* anxiety.

CHAPTER 2

A DIFFERENT KIND OF CONVERSATION

Think back to a time in your own life when things were painful or dark. Ask yourself what you needed most in those moments. Was it someone to come and 'solve' it for you? Was it someone to encourage you to look at things in a different light?

These approaches might have helped at a later point. But most of the time when we are distressed, and at our most vulnerable, what we need most is for someone to get alongside us in solidarity, and listen without judgement.

"If you have been fortunate enough
to be listened to fully and completely,
you will know what a powerful
experience it is."

THE LOST ART OF LISTENING

In our world of group chats, scrolling and endless demands competing for our attention, it is increasingly rare to sit down one-to-one, and have an open conversation. When we do manage to make time for each other, our desire to solve or fix can get in the way of truly listening, without an agenda.

If you have been fortunate enough to be listened to fully and completely, you will know what a powerful experience it is.

At the age of 21, I had completed my psychology degree and started counselling training. In the initial weeks, as part of a personal development group, each trainee had to share their life story.

On an October afternoon, sitting on old, wooden, classroom-style chairs, in a group of about 12 relative strangers (or new friends, as it turned out), it was my turn to tell my story. I probably spoke for about ten minutes, uninterrupted. When I finished, the group facilitator gently reflected some of the things I had shared. She didn't challenge anything I had said; she didn't ask me to think about it differently, or to consider anyone else. She didn't suggest my feelings about anything should be different, or offer me an alternative perspective. Her response continued like that for a few minutes, and then other group members joined in, responding in the same way. From their words, I could see that they had not only heard what I

2 A DIFFERENT KIND OF CONVERSATION

said, but they were willing to meet me in it; no ifs, no buts, no what-abouts.

I waited for the other shoe to drop. It never did.

It wasn't that I had not had good people around me before that; I had. What was new was the willingness to listen without the 'Yes, but'. What was new was the total dedication, in that moment, to hearing my experience, and mine only.

I have gone on to experience different types of therapy, different ways of making sense of my experience, and picked up tools and techniques that have helped massively in my life. But nothing – nothing – has ever made more of a difference than being heard, met and validated in my experience, without judgement or agenda.

"If you want to make a difference to someone who is suffering, this is the most important piece of advice in the whole book: Listen. Listen fully."

When I reach the end of therapy with clients, I usually ask them for a bit of feedback. One thing comes back with resounding consistency: having the space to talk, and to be met in a safe, validating and non-judgemental space, is among the most helpful things we can offer a person who is struggling.

Of course, it is not possible for us to create a full and intense experience of listening to one another every time we communicate in our day-to-day lives. Real life relationships and everyday conversations are reciprocal, often hurried, and complex.

But if you picked up this book because you want to make a difference to someone who is suffering, this is the most important piece of advice in the whole book. Listen. Listen fully. Take time, be willing to hear what the person has to say. Suspend any urge to judge or to fix. Just listen.

Whether it is in person, online, over the phone, or in some other way, connection is at the heart of the helping relationship.

This book contains techniques and ideas to help you support someone with anxiety to be empowered. But without the foundation of having listened – and continuing to listen – to the person you are seeking to help, your intervention could put more distance between you, not less. If you go ahead and try to offer tools and solutions without first having properly listened, you risk leaving the other person feeling misunderstood and disempowered.

THE FIVE LEVELS OF LISTENING

Do you sometimes have conversations where you are speaking – maybe sharing an idea or a story – and you can tell that the other person is just not listening? Have you ever sat in a meeting where someone has taken out their laptop and started checking email? Have you started telling an anecdote to be interrupted suddenly with an unrelated story or point?

Sometimes the signs of disengagement from a conversation are clear. When the other person constantly breaks their connection with you, to look at their phone, for example, you know that you do not have their undivided attention.

Sometimes the signs whether or not someone is engaged in listening are more subtle. They might appear to be listening to you, only for it to be revealed later that they have not taken in any of the important detail of what you were saying.

In his book *The 7 Habits of Highly Effective People*, Stephen Covey sets out what he believes are the five levels of listening.[iv] As we go through these, take a moment to reflect on your own experience of being on the receiving end of each level. Notice what feelings come up as you recall interactions in which you may have felt ignored, or that listening was superficial.

Covey's model of listening has its origins in leadership and business, but the principles are relevant to how we listen within a helping relationship, or any other relationship.

Level 1 – Ignoring

We all know the feeling of being ignored. It is the feeling we get when we detect that we do not have the other person's attention in the conversation. When listening at this level, we may pick up the basics of what someone is talking about, but we are not engaged at a meaningful level, and our attention is elsewhere.

Level 2 – Pretending

Sometimes, we might be in a conversation where we think we are being listened to because the person is giving some signs of engagement, like nodding or uttering short words of encouragement. However, we later realize that they have not taken in any of what we were saying. When we listen at this level, we manage to look like we are listening (at least in part), but our attention remains elsewhere.

Level 3 – Selective

This is when the listener is looking out for certain things in the conversation, without taking in all of what is being said. Sometimes, when we are opening up to someone about a problem, we might find that they are selectively looking out for a 'positive', or a way to redirect our thinking. When they spot that, they may jump in and focus on that part, without taking in the broader conversation.

When we are in a helping role, it is easy to fall into this level of listening, because we may think that we know what is best for the other person, or think we know what they need. That can mean that we selectively search for certain things when they speak, so that we can use that to move them to our way of thinking. By doing so without listening to the full picture, we risk missing the point, or the emotion, of what the other person is saying.

Level 4 – Attentive

When we are listening attentively, we are focused on the other person, and taking in all of what they are saying. At this level, we are engaged, and have a good chance of creating a connection that allows for a constructive conversation.

Level 5 – Empathic

This level goes beyond attentive listening because it involves an emotional connection with what the other person is saying. It involves not only paying attention and taking in what is being said, but being able to relate to the other person's experience as if it were happening to us. This is the listening level at which deep connection can occur. When empathic listening is achieved, it sets an excellent foundation for a helping relationship.

In the next chapter we will look in more detail at empathy, and what steps you can take to foster an empathic connection with the person you wish to support.

HOW TO HELP

- Become aware of your usual level of listening by checking in with yourself during conversations.
- Notice if you tend to become easily distracted, butt in, or are always waiting for your chance to give your perspective.
- Remember good listening is not about waiting for your turn to speak; it is about hearing and connecting with the other person.
- Challenge yourself to achieve a higher level of listening by keeping focused on the other person, and seeking to hear them without interruption or bias (I know this is hard, but don't worry – we are going to work on this a lot more in the next chapter).
- Remember you can listen at a distance by speaking online or on the phone. The modality is not the important thing; connection is what matters.

A FRAMEWORK FOR HELPING

Now that we have recognized that listening is the first step toward helping someone with anxiety, I want to introduce a framework that you can use to remind yourself of how to set up a different conversation with them.

Throughout the book, we are going to refer to the acronym TURN, which brings together the key elements of helping that we will work through together. This framework can be used as a practical step-by-step approach for helping someone with anxiety.

TURN stands for the following:

TIME

The first, and probably the most important, thing you can do for the person you are supporting is to give them your time. Time is the foundation on which we can build listening, connection and a sense of shared purpose.

UNDERSTANDING

It is one thing to listen and empathize with the person you want to help. That, in itself, is a powerful way of providing support. But to take that further, the experience of anxiety can be broken down into its components, to get a deeper understanding of what is going on for the other person.

REFRAMING AND REDIRECTING

Once you have spent time with the person you are helping to hear and understand what is going on for them, you can consider offering ways of making sense of things slightly differently, or ways of behaving a bit differently. This can be a powerful approach for creating a shift in anxiety.

NEW APPROACH

Good coping strategies are essential for living well with anxiety. Once you and the person with anxiety have a good, shared understanding of what is going on, and you are working on trying different ways of thinking and acting in the presence of anxiety, you may find it helpful to try out some new techniques and approaches for better coping.

This framework will form the basis of how we approach learning to help someone with anxiety. We will work through each of the elements in detail as we move through the different stages of the book.

SUMMARY

- The most important thing you can do to help someone with anxiety is to listen.
- Listening attentively, and with empathy, takes practice.
- The TURN framework is a step-by-step approach to helping someone with anxiety:
  - **T**ime
  - **U**nderstanding
  - **R**eframing and Redirecting
  - **N**ew Approach

CHAPTER 3

LEARNING THE ART OF LISTENING

Catriona's parents, Robert and Angela, have looked on with concern since they learned that Catriona was struggling with anxiety. They were full of hope and optimism when their daughter set off for university. She did so well at school and, from their perspective, has nothing to fear when it comes to her academic ability or exam performance. It took them by surprise when she finally shared with them how difficult she has found life at university.

When the subject of exams comes up, Robert and Angela do their best to try and reassure Catriona that she has nothing to worry about. They try to refer back to her various successes at school and earlier university years, to help Catriona feel less anxious about her ability.

As time goes on and Catriona has continued to struggle, both Robert and Angela have been getting more and more worried. On a couple of occasions, they have told her it is time to pull herself together and get through the exams with less of a fuss. When that approach has caused Catriona to get even more distressed, they have backed away, feeling guilty, helpless and lost.

TAKE YOUR TIME AND GIVE YOUR TIME

It is one thing to notice that someone close to you is suffering, but another to help them get to the point where they feel able to share that experience with you. Ultimately, you will not be able to control if, when and how someone chooses to open up. What you *can* control is how you make yourself available, and how you show your willingness to listen, when the other person is ready to invite you in.

"Take your Time. Go gently, slow the pace, and ease into the conversation."

When we see that someone is suffering, it can be tempting to push them to open up by constantly broaching the subject, or making lots of suggestions about what they could do to improve their situation. While this might be done with the best of intentions, this approach risks putting additional pressure on the other person, and making them less likely to feel safe enough to engage and talk honestly, on their own terms.

The first step in the TURN method (see page 29) is TIME. That is, giving the person you are supporting your time, so that they have an opportunity to talk to you, and that you have the opportunity to listen. It also stands for TAKE your TIME. In other words, go gently, slow the pace, and ease into the conversation.

If the other person is not yet willing to talk, it can be tempting to move to offering new perspectives. In other words, it can be tempting to skip the listening and jump straight to the active 'helping'. While this approach is well-meant, it risks listening at the selective level, rather than the empathic level (see pages 26 and 27). For empathic listening, you must listen in full and without an agenda, rather than looking for your opportunity to jump in and suggest an alternative perspective.

It takes patience, and consistency, but the best thing you can do is continue to offer your time, and to let the person experiencing anxiety know that you want to give them your full attention, whenever they are ready to open up. Be upfront about your desire to help, but make it clear that you are prepared to respect their pace.

Your time, alone, is probably the most helpful thing you can give someone who is suffering, struggling or in distress. That is time without distraction; offering your undivided attention.

In our busy lives, this can require consciously putting aside time to listen. In order to listen attentively, and empathically, we need to be *present* with the other person. And this can involve prioritizing that over other things that might compete for our time.

When the person you want to help indicates they are distressed, give your time immediately if you can. If that is not possible, agree with them when you will put time aside to spend

HOW TO HELP

- Start at the beginning of the TURN framework, by giving your TIME and taking your TIME.
- Recognize that giving your time is an essential step toward helping someone with anxiety.
- Prioritize time with the person you are supporting when you can give them your full attention without interruptions or distractions.
- State your intention to the other person. Let them know that you want to spend time with them, and that you want to give your attention to hearing about what they are going through, if they are willing to share that.
- Get rid of distractions: turn off the TV, put your phone away, sit still, and offer your undivided attention to the other person for the duration of the conversation.
- Refer back to the five levels of listening (see page 24) and consider on what level you are engaging.

listening to them properly, by sitting down with them face-to-face, or to speak online or over the phone when you will not be disturbed. This, in itself, is one of the most important steps toward setting up a different kind of conversation.

HOW TO OPEN UP THE CONVERSATION

"Your humanity, and your shared humanity with the person you are supporting, is your most important asset."

It can be difficult to know how to start up a new kind of conversation, especially if subjects like mental health and anxiety feel awkward or uncomfortable.

Here are some ways you can try out for opening up the conversation:

- 'I can see that you are struggling, and I am here to listen.'
- 'You can speak to me about it any time.'
- 'I am no expert, but I would like to help you work it out if I can.'
- 'Tell me what it is like for you.'
- 'Let's try to make sense of it together.'

BEING VULNERABLE

When we invite someone to talk to us about their difficulties, we are inviting them to talk to us about something real. And if we expect someone to be real and vulnerable with us, we need to be prepared to be real and vulnerable in return.

Before tools, techniques or wise words must come shared humanity. Your humanity, and your shared humanity with the person you are supporting, is your most important asset for opening up a different kind of conversation.

I am talking about going into the conversation with an open heart. We cannot expect someone to trust us with their suffering if we are not willing to be touched by what they tell us. In order to do that, we need to be prepared to lay aside urges to know better or offer solutions. We need to lay aside any perception we may have of ourselves as a saviour or hero in the situation.

If you can get into the space of shared humanity, of not knowing the answers, of being prepared to get it wrong and fail, and try again, you are in the best possible position to build a connection where the other person feels safe enough to be able to trust and open up. Being real, authentic and getting it wrong occasionally will get you a lot further than being clever, and having all the answers.

When someone shares a situation or a perspective with us, it can be natural to want to challenge it, especially if we see things differently to them. But, in order to build confidence and trust, it is important that you suspend the urge to interrupt, correct or offer an alternative point of view. For someone to feel safe sharing with you, they need to know that their experience will be validated.

Providing validation is not about *agreeing* or *disagreeing* with the other person's perspective. Validation comes from recognizing how the other person, and affirming that by taking their perspective on board, without challenge. You may go on to help the other person shift their perspective later on, but at the initial listening stage it is important to show that you recognize their perspective as valid, understandable and worthwhile. Later on in the chapter, we will look at ways you can communicate in a validating way.

If the person you are seeking to help detects impatience and frustration from you, or feels pressured to change, they are more likely to shut down. By contrast, an attitude of patience and openness sets the context for a safe and trusting conversation.

For Robert and Angela, hearing Catriona doubt her own abilities was difficult because they perceived her as capable, and were able to see an abundance of evidence for that. With good intentions, they tried to remind Catriona of the evidence of her ability, and to emphasize all her past achievements, when Catriona shared her fear and self-doubt. Catriona knows her parents mean well. But instead of helping her feel better, their approach leaves her thinking no one understands. This makes her feel even more anxious, isolated and alone.

HOW TO HELP

- When the person you want to support shares their experience with you, listen to them without interrupting.
- In the first instance, prioritize allowing the person you are supporting to speak, over sharing your perspective or suggestions.
- Show your engagement without interrupting. You can do this by keeping eye contact, nodding and focusing your attention on what is being said.
- Reflect back what the person tells you. Pick up on their language to describe anxiety, and use the same language when you respond.
- Always validate first. You might see a great opportunity to challenge the other person, or offer them a different perspective. Listen and validate before you consider offering a new perspective. (Remember the order of the TURN method!)
- Resist the urge to jump in when there is a gap. Allow space and silence in the conversation.
- Remember your purpose is to explore, not to fix.
- Resist any urge to encourage the person you are

supporting to 'look on the bright side'. Meet them in their distress before introducing a different perspective.

- Be particularly careful if you find yourself saying, 'At least it's not …' or 'Things could be worse.' You may be offering this perspective with the best of intentions, but you risk minimizing what the other person is going through.
- Be yourself. Ultimately, you will have your own way of showing willingness and curiosity.
- Remember: your humanity is your best asset.

EXAMPLES OF WHAT TO SAY

Some useful questions to ask someone with anxiety:

- 'What does it feel like when that happens?'
- 'Tell me more about what that's like.'
- 'What is the most important thing for me to understand about what it's like for you?'

Some ways of communicating validation:

- 'I can see how it would feel like that.'
- 'That sounds so scary/painful/difficult.'
- 'I get it.'

"Be prepared to open yourself up to a deeper connection with the other person, by not just hearing their words, but stepping in to their experience as if it were your own, and feeling it as if it were your own. That is empathy."

WALK A MILE IN THEIR SHOES

When I talk about listening, I don't mean listening just to hear and make sense of what the other person is telling you. Of course, the factual information and the detail of what they share is important, but what is often more important is the emotion the other person shares. This is what takes us from attentive listening to empathic listening.

To listen for emotion, you need to be prepared to listen with your body. That means noticing what happens for you when the person close to you shares their distress. It means noticing what urges or feelings come up in you while you take in what they are saying. It means being prepared to open yourself up to a deeper connection with the other person, which involves not just hearing their words, but temporarily stepping in to their experience as if it were your own, and feeling it as if it were your own. That is empathy.

When we can relate to an experience or a story as if it were *our* experience or story, our response tends to be deeper and more authentic. When we are able to let the other person see that we 'get' where they are, and what that experience is like for them, we deepen the connection. And a deeper connection is, in itself, a powerful space for healing, growth and empowerment.

I GET IT

Think about a time in your own life when you have talked about something painful or difficult with someone, and you have felt like the other person just got it. They got the full meaning of what you talked about, and you could tell by the way they responded to you in the conversation. It's a good feeling isn't it? There are few things as powerful in communication as feeling completely understood.

Having been through a similar experience is one way of connecting with what that thing might be like for someone else. And if the other person knows that we, too, have 'been there', that can give the conversation a basis of shared understanding. This is not necessarily about sharing your own experience with the other person in any level of detail, and it is certainly not about redirecting the conversation to focus on your own issues. This is about letting the other person see that you can relate to their experience.

And if you have not been in the same position as the person you are seeking to help – if you have never really struggled with anxiety in the way that they are – you may have other experiences that you can draw from to help you get it.

You can probably 'get' anxiety, at least to some extent, if you have ever experienced any of the following:

- Felt like you won't be able to cope when something goes wrong.
- Faced uncertainty and expected the worst.
- Felt overwhelmed with life's demands.
- Wanted to try something but felt too scared.
- Lost something that mattered to you.
- Held on to something because you were afraid what would happen if you let go.
- Hidden away, been humiliated, felt left out, or feared you might not be good enough.

"Empathy tells the other person that you can relate to their emotional experience."

Your experience does not have to be the same as that of the person you are supporting for you to 'get it'. Tuning in to your own experience of pain, fear, anxiety or self-doubt will not replicate for you what is going on for the other person, but it can tune you in to some of the emotions that might be going on for them. And if you can feel those emotions, you will be in a better position to get it, truthfully and with empathy.

It is not about being able to say, 'I know how you feel.' In fact, even if you have been in exactly the same position as the person you want to support, it does not necessarily mean you know how they feel, because we all respond differently.

HOW TO HELP

- Be prepared to reflect on your own experiences of anxiety. This is not necessarily to share the details of your own experience, but to help you relate to how someone with anxiety might be feeling.
- Reflect emotions back to the person you are supporting. If you recognize their struggle and their pain, tell them.
- Seek to empathize with the other person's emotions, and to validate the emotions they share with you.
- Some more ways of communicating validation and empathy could be:
  - 'That sounds so hard.'
  - 'I can't say I have had that exact experience, but I know what fear feels like.'
  - 'I hear you.'
  - 'I am sorry it has been so awful.'

Empathy tells the other person that you can relate to their emotional experience. Anyone who has been met with empathy knows what a powerful force it is for putting you at ease and creating safety, when you might otherwise feel too vulnerable or alone to share how you are feeling.

I'VE BEEN THERE

There was a time in my own life when I was going through a loss so sad that I did not know how I would go forward. People around me did what they could to be supportive, but most words seemed empty to me in my sadness.

An acquaintance who had come to know of my circumstances came to speak to me. They spoke only a few words, but what they said was enough to tell me two things: they had been where I was, and they had come through it. My pain was understandable; there was hope. Choice words from a relative stranger, loaded with empathy and hope, helped me more at that time than any amount of sympathy, or any practical offerings.

But, equally, there will be times when being met with 'I've been there' can leave us feeling dismissed, misunderstood and lonely.

Here is the trickiest balance in helping someone with a difficult emotional experience. How useful is it to share something you have been through?

"By offering your own story, you join the other person in their vulnerability."

If you are considering sharing something from your own life, take some time to think about the purpose of sharing. If you have been able to give time and attention to the other person's story, and there is something from you own life that resonated strongly, and has the potential to help the other person, sharing might be a good idea.

Making a decision about how much to share can be a tricky balance. Hearing that you have been there could help the person you want to support feel safer and more able to share.

By offering your own story, you join the other person in their vulnerability. This can be a powerful way of levelling the playing field, and deepening the connection not just for the conversation, but for the whole relationship.

Hearing that you have been there can go a long way toward normalizing anxiety, and break down any stigma the other person might feel about their struggles. Hearing someone else has had a similar experience can cut through any sense of being the only one who struggles, and shame that might be attached to that.

It is not about saying 'Don't think you're the only one; lots of people have problems'; it is about saying 'You're not alone – these feelings do not make you strange, broken or beyond help.'

If your story has a positive outcome, or there are particular things you learned that could empower the person you want to support, sharing could be a powerful way of relating and providing hope.

It may be that there was something that really helped you when you were in a similar position, that you think could help your loved one too. By all means, go on to share that later (while remembering that not everything works in the same way for everyone).

HOW TO HELP

Before you share your own experience, it can be useful to reflect on why you are sharing. You can ask yourself:

- Am I interrupting?
- Am I 'knowing it all'?
- Has the person that I am supporting finished talking about their experience?
- Could my story help build trust, show empathy or provide hope?
- Do I feel OK to share this in a conversation that is not about me, but about helping someone else?

If you do decide to go ahead and share something from your own experience, make sure you listen fully and completely to the person you are supporting first. Always prioritize listening to sharing your own story, and if in doubt, stick with listening.

Always remember: your experience is not the same as that of the other person. If it feels right, offer your experience as a gateway to a deeper conversation, but make sure you maintain focus on the person you are helping, and let them know that the conversation is about them, not about you.

Catriona had always seen her father, Robert, as being cool, calm and in control. When she first shared some of her anxiety struggles with him, she was not surprised that he seemed frustrated. After all, what would he know about anxiety, self-doubt and fear of failure?

Catriona appreciated her parents' efforts to build her confidence by reminding her of her achievements. But if it was that simple, she could do that for herself. The moment things changed for Catriona was when her dad sat down with her and asked her what anxiety was like for her.

Robert listened carefully as Catriona described the crippling fear she felt every time she was asked a question or had to hand in a piece of work.

'I know how that feels,' he said, as she described her sense of not being clever enough to be at university.

This simple disclosure opened the door for Catriona to express surprise that Robert would know that feeling, and for Robert to share some of his own self-doubt. It took Catriona's breath away to know that her dad – who always seemed so together, and so in command – could struggle with feelings of inadequacy and self-doubt. For Catriona, that was more powerful than any advice or tools he could have offered. Robert's human struggle was the gateway to a deeper conversation about Catriona's difficulties, and what she wanted to change.

YOU CAN'T FORCE POSITIVITY

When someone close to us shares something painful or difficult, our natural instinct is to try to make things better for them. Our urge is to be positive. Part of us might believe that if we are cheerful, or model 'good coping', the other person will follow suit and break out of their anxiety. We have all done it: told someone to 'cheer up,' 'calm down' or 'be positive' when we have wanted to help them change their mindset.

Being *positive* is often viewed as a desirable quality, or a welcome perspective. But it is important to be aware that, in some contexts, jumping to positivity can mean we badly miss the mark for empathic listening and deep connection.

Of course, hope is important. But when someone is in despair or in the grip of anxiety, it is unlikely that a cheery, positive approach that overlooks their suffering will help them feel empowered or inspire connection. Denying someone's emotions in this way – even if done with the best of intentions – can set back the development of trust and safety between you.

> "One of the most important skills in listening is this: being OK with things being difficult, without immediately jumping in to make things 'better'."

One of the most important skills in listening is this: being OK with things being difficult, without immediately jumping in to make things 'better'. The much more powerful alternative is to meet the other person fully in their pain, and sitting in that pain with them.

Having said that, there is an important difference between empathizing with another person and becoming engulfed by the emotional experience they might share with you. There is a balance between maintaining your own sense of hope and possibility, while being open to feeling the other person's pain.

This is a difficult thing to do, and the emotional toll of that is not something to be overlooked. We will talk later in the book about ways in which you, as the helper, can manage this balance and put loving boundaries in place to protect your own wellbeing.

HOW TO HELP

- Be willing to go to where the pain is, and meet the other person there. That means tolerating the discomfort of sitting with difficult emotions.
- Avoid overly positive responses that could deny the other person's suffering.
- Here are some examples of 'positivity' that could invalidate how someone else is feeling:
  - 'You have so much to be grateful for. Try focusing on that.'
  - 'Try not to take everything so seriously.'
  - 'Smile. You have such a lovely smile.'
  - 'At least you still have a job/ it's not a physical illness/ the kids are OK.'
  - 'Try to look on the bright side.'
  - 'It could be worse! Plenty of people are worse off.'

SUMMARY

- Give your TIME to listen, and take your TIME in the conversation. Proceed gently, and only with the other person's consent.
- Be prepared to open yourself up to your loved one's emotional pain, and to meet them in their suffering.
- Before you offer any challenge, tool or strategy, make sure you have listened fully, without judgement and without trying to 'fix'.
- Let go of the need for things to be 'better', or to position yourself as the 'expert'.
- Go to where the pain is, remembering it hurts because it matters. Talking about difficult things does not make things worse.

CHAPTER 4

FORMING AN UNDERSTANDING

George had experienced a degree of anxiety for as long as he could remember. He would fear the worst when travelling, or when members of his family were away. His mind was prone to jumping to the worst-case scenario and taunting him with thoughts and images about what might go wrong.

Since retiring from his job in the police force, George finds that anxiety is playing a bigger and bigger role in his life. He finds that he is more stressed and anxious about day-to-day things like home repairs, or minor disagreements with his wife. New or unexpected things have become increasingly difficult because he thinks that he somehow will not be able to manage problems or cope with stressful situations.

George has noticed that when his anxiety is triggered his body becomes rigid with fear, and he can feel his heart racing. He becomes hot and sweaty and struggles to think straight. This is a big concern for George because he worries about his health. Sometimes he thinks there is something seriously wrong with him. He goes online to research what could be causing hot flushes and muddled thinking. This ends up making him panic even more.

George worries constantly about his grown-up children, and phones them a number of times a day to check that they are OK. If he is not able to contact them, he becomes agitated and panicked.

George's wife Helen does her best to reassure him. She encourages their son and daughter to be in touch with their dad as much as possible to minimize his anxiety. Helen makes sure she keeps any problems or bad news from George to stop his anxiety getting worse. Helen has started making excuses when she and George are invited out with friends, because she does not want to cause George any undue stress. All she wants is for his anxiety to be gone.

The second step in the TURN framework is UNDERSTANDING. In this chapter, we are going to look at how you can help the person you are supporting gain an understanding of their experience of anxiety.

When we face a difficult situation, the surge of strong emotions can feel overwhelming. When we are engulfed by emotion, it can be difficult to see that this experience is made up of interacting components and patterns.

By taking a step back and observing, we can identify the various components of an emotional response. Getting to know the components and patterns that play a part in our experience can be an essential step toward better managing anxiety.

In therapy, one way we work on getting a handle on difficult emotions is by making sense of what triggers those emotions. Once we know what can trigger difficult emotions, we can begin to identify patterns that influence how these emotions develop and unfold.

Before we can influence or change a pattern, we need to understand how that pattern is formed.

IT BEGINS WITH THE BODY

In therapy, getting a full understanding of how threat affects our bodies can be one of the most empowering steps on the journey to better managing anxiety.

When our threat system is activated and the *whoosh* of anxiety hits us (see page 6), it can feel like our bodies are breaking down and our minds are not thinking straight. In the midst of that, we may feel so engulfed by anxiety that it is difficult to see a way through it. This is the force of the anxiety storm.

In this section, we are going to look at the physical events that play out to create the experience we know as anxiety. I hope this knowledge will give you some insight into the physical basis of anxiety, and how that might be experienced by the person you want to support.

As you go through this section, it may be useful to think about your own experience of anxiety, and see whether you can relate to the physical experiences described. You can also check whether these physical effects are familiar to the person you are supporting. Remember: taking time and listening should come first (see Chapter 3). Understanding is the step that follows.

A STORM BREWING

When our threat system – or our inner 'fire alarm' – is activated, it triggers a physical reaction as if we are facing real and immediate physical danger with a threat of harm or a threat to survival. The fire alarm always sends the same signal; it has no range. There's simply danger or no danger.

The responses that it triggers in the body are geared to prepare us to keep ourselves safe in primitive terms; that is, to fight off or run away from a predator. And whether we are going to be engaging in a fight or we are going to be running, our threat system anticipates that we are going to be engaging in some form of physical exertion.

So, the response that is triggered prepares us to literally fight or flight; to fight off a predator or to run away from it. The body reacts to set us up for physical exertion and energize us enough to be able to keep ourselves safe. It does a number of key things to give us the best possible chance in our upcoming fight or run. Whether the smoke detector has been triggered, or someone has come along and smashed the glass, the warning signal is now sounding loud and clear. This happens automatically, and instantly upon detection of threat. From that point, our body prepares to act quickly.

Our internal fire signal goes like this:

- Adrenaline floods the body, giving us a shot of energy. Adrenaline is like a fuel that optimizes our physical performance under stress. When adrenaline is running, we are primed for physical action. Muscles tense to give us strength and resistance.
- The heart works harder and faster to pump blood to our muscles.
- Our breathing speeds up and we take in more air, bringing extra oxygen into the bloodstream.
- The brain redeploys some of its own resources to support the body to fight or run away. It does this by taking blood and oxygen from parts of the brain that are not necessarily critical in a life or death situation, and redistributing those resources to the bodily functions that are imperative in keeping us safe in an emergency.

- Physical functions not immediately essential to survival – such as the digestive system – are put on standby, and their resources are redeployed to where they are needed most.

This is exactly what you would want your body to do if you were being chased by a big angry dog or a bear. The increased flow of blood and oxygen would help you run faster for longer, or fight more effectively. Your body's resources would be exactly where you needed them to keep you safe, and this would be done for you with no conscious thought or decision-making.

ALL DRESSED UP WITH NOWHERE TO GO

But, of course, this primal bodily response is not always a good fit for modern life and circumstances. The system that we are born with, and can probably be credited for having kept us safe on some occasions, can play another, less helpful, role in our lives.

What happens if our smoke detector is overly sensitive? What happens when it is prone to activating the fire alarm when there is little or no immediate threat or danger?

The smoke detector does not contain a function that makes it stop sounding if there is no actual fire. And just like that, the physical fight-or-flight response does not automatically stop or cancel itself out when it realizes that we are not running or fighting for our lives.

This means that if the body is not exerted, we end up with a big shot of energy that has no outlet. We are geared up to fight or run for our lives, but there is no one for us to fight and nothing to run from. Our physical systems are all dressed up with nowhere to go.

This situation generates a number of physical experiences, some of which may be familiar.

Breathing changes: In normal circumstances, we only need to breathe in more oxygen when we are physically exerted – when we naturally become out of breath. When this happens, we also breathe out more air, so the extra oxygen coming in is balanced by the increased carbon dioxide being breathed out. When we breathe in more oxygen due to the fear response, however, we don't produce enough carbon dioxide to balance it out, so we can feel lightheaded and dizzy, and have difficulty focusing until our breathing regulates again.

Changes in thinking: The redeployment of the body's resources means that the function of the parts of the brain that deal with rational thinking and planning is temporarily reduced. In practical terms, that means our ability to think straight, to be coherent, and to logically and sequentially follow a plan can be temporarily impaired. Our thoughts may race, and it may feel more difficult to connect with our rational, logical perspective.

Digestive changes: The digestive system is another area that is put on standby in a threatening situation. Reduced resources

"When we put together the physical and mental effects of the body's strategies that prepare us to protect ourselves, a familiar picture emerges."

in that area can create the feeling of butterflies or lurching in the stomach, and sometimes create the need to go to the toilet urgently. Changes in the digestive system can also cause the mouth to dry up temporarily.

Sweating: One effect of increased blood flow is that it causes the body to warm up and become hot. To compensate for this, the body sweats to cool itself down.

So, you can see that the body has a brilliant range of strategies to prepare us to act quickly and protect ourselves in the face of threat, but when we put together the physical and mental effects of these strategies, a familiar picture emerges:

- Racing heart
- Faster breathing
- Tension in the muscles
- Lurching in the stomach
- Urgently needing the toilet
- Thoughts racing or mind going blank
- Not able to think straight

- Dry mouth
- Feeling hot
- Sweating
- Becoming dizzy or lightheaded

In George's case, physical experiences play an important part in anxiety storms. When George's mind hijacks him with a worst-case scenario, his fight-or-flight mechanism is activated. His mind gives him an anxiety-provoking 'what if' situation, and immediately the smoke alarm is triggered.

For George, that triggers a physical experience of feeling hot, becoming sweaty, and temporarily losing clarity of thought.

Looking at this situation objectively, it is clear to see that these physical changes are likely to be occurring because George's body is responding to a perceived threat.

HOW TO HELP

- When you seek to understand someone's experience of anxiety, remember that anxiety has a strong physical element.
- Look at the physical effects of the fight-or-flight response with the person you are supporting. Support

them to explore which physical responses they
recognize as being linked to their anxiety.

- Use your understanding of the fight-or-flight response
to help the other person see the physical side of
anxiety as a natural and normal part of how the body
deals with threat. Understanding the physical side
of anxiety can be an important step in becoming
empowered to manage the experience.

THE ANATOMY OF AN ANXIETY STORM

At any given time, our experience is made up of a number of
interweaving factors.

*As George's case illustrates, anxiety is not solely a physical
experience. Thought processes and behaviour make up
other influential parts of the picture. These factors interact,
and do so rapidly, creating an intensifying storm of anxiety.*

For the purposes of helping you and the person you want to
support work together to seek a better understanding of their
anxiety, I want to introduce you to a framework that comes from
Cognitive Behavioural Therapy, or CBT.

CBT is a therapeutic approach created by Aaron Beck, a psychologist, in the 1960s. His approach, and various adaptations of it, are widely applied in the treatment of anxiety.

Using part of the theory on which CBT is based,[v] we can break down an anxiety storm into five components. Breaking things down in this way allows us to step back from the storm and reduce the overwhelm it creates.

The five components we are going to look at are:

1. The situation (what happened)
2. Thoughts (how we make sense of what happened)
3. Feelings (our emotional response)
4. The body (our physical response)
5. Behaviour (what we do or do not do in response)

Although these components are separate, they are all linked. In every individual situation, each component influences and feeds off the other, creating feedback loops. It is the repetition of feedback loops between the five components that escalates the anxiety storm.

When we feel anxious, we are more likely to think about things that make us feel anxious. We are more likely to recall anxiety-provoking memories, and to focus on things that we are worried about. We get into a loop where we think more anxious thoughts, so we feel more anxious, so we think even more anxious thoughts, and we feel even more anxious. When we are in the grip of this process, anxiety can escalate rapidly, to the point that it becomes overwhelming.

> "Breaking down what goes on in an anxiety storm can help us understand anxiety better."

Sometimes, by the time we are aware of what is going on, we have reached a highly anxious and panicked state. By that point, we may be feeling stuck and hopeless, because the distress is so intense and all-encompassing.

Breaking down what goes on in an anxiety storm into these five components can help us understand anxiety better.

Identifying the five components is in itself an empowering part of understanding an anxiety storm. What may be even more important is recognizing the relationship between the various components, as shown in the diagram on page 64, adapted from a model developed and made popular by Christine Padesky – an innovator and leader in the field of CBT.[vi]

Notice that the arrows between each of the four central components point both ways.

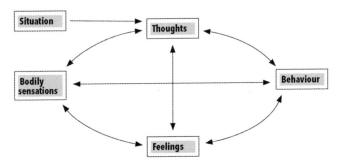

Thoughts affect feelings, but equally, feelings affect thoughts. The body is affected by each of these components, and each of these components influence what happens in the body.

Behaviour is influenced by the combination of thoughts, feelings and bodily responses. Behaviour then feeds back in a loop, further influencing thoughts, emotions and physical experiences.

In this diagram, the arrows are just as important as each of the individual components of the system. The arrows illustrate the bi-directional relationships between the components. You can see how each component feeds back into the others, creating a powerful feedback loop.

THE THOUGHT–FEELING LINK

Sometimes, thoughts and feelings can seem so entwined that it is difficult to distinguish which is which. In therapy, I often spend time with clients exploring and clarifying this important difference.

Our thoughts are how we make sense of a situation. Often, the types of thoughts that feature in anxiety storms are thoughts relating to us being threatened or unsafe in some way. That might be thoughts about threat to our safety, our sense of self, potential success or failure, or relationships.

Thoughts can be opinions, assumptions or predictions relating to ourselves, other people or the world in general. The way we think about situations in the moment is often influenced by our existing beliefs. We will explore thoughts and beliefs in a lot more depth in the next chapter.

'Feelings' refer to the physical and emotional sensations we get when something moves us, in a positive or a negative way. Thoughts and feelings are very closely linked because the way we think about something directly shapes how it affects us emotionally. In turn, our emotional state influences our thinking.

Here are some examples of the types of the thoughts I commonly hear from people who are experiencing anxiety:

- 'This is going to go wrong.'
- 'I won't be able to cope.'
- 'I look like an idiot.'
- 'My ideas will be rubbish compared to everyone else.'
- 'I am going to get seriously ill.'
- 'Everyone is laughing at me.'
- 'I will be abandoned/rejected/forgotten.'

Some of the emotions that often form part of anxiety storms include:

- Anxiety (of course!)
- Fear
- Terror
- Panic
- Nervousness
- Embarrassment
- Shame

The way in which we think about a situation – or the way we interpret a situation – directly influences the feelings that occur.

Here's an example: you are walking down the street in daylight when you pass a neighbour who is out walking her dog on the other side of the road. You see your neighbour and raise your hand to wave. Your neighbour does not make eye contact, and keeps on walking without acknowledging you.

What is your response? Well, that might depend on how you make sense of what has just happened. Here are three interpretations:

Interpretation 1: 'Oh no, I must have said something to offend my neighbour the last time we spoke. I have obviously done something wrong and now she is not speaking to me.'

That interpretation might trigger you to feel anxious, ashamed or apprehensive.

Interpretation 2: 'How rude! I went out of my way to be friendly and I didn't get as much as an acknowledgement. Some people have no manners!'

The tone of this interpretation is quite different and you might feel affronted, angry or outraged.

Interpretation 3: 'There goes my neighbour. She is not wearing her glasses. I suppose she did not see me.'

How does it feel now with this further perspective?

The emotional experience, and the extent to which we detect threat, is heavily influenced by how we make sense of what is going on in our environment. In other words, our feelings about a situation are largely determined by what *meaning* we give that situation.

THE BODY AND BEHAVIOUR

The first interpretation was perhaps the anxiety-provoking one – you thought that your neighbour had deliberately ignored you because you had offended her, and the emotional response was anxiety and shame. In other words, the interpretation triggered a threat response.

Let's think about what might happen next. The threat response could mean activation of the fight-or-flight mechanism. You might feel a wave of heat come over your body. You might struggle to think straight. You might put your head down, look the other way, and start walking faster. For the rest of the day, you might be hijacked by thoughts about what happened.

"Our thoughts, feelings and physical responses are closely linked and are also connected to our behaviour."

Following that, what would happen the next time you saw your neighbour? Based on the earlier negative experience, you may seek to avoid coming into contact with her. You might avoid going out if you saw her passing, or even avoid going out at times when you knew she was likely to be going down the street.

Our thoughts, feelings and physical responses are closely linked and are also connected to our behaviour.

The role of behaviour in anxiety is something we are going to look at in detail later on in the book. But for now, I want to highlight that there is often a difference between what we *intend* when we use behaviour to manage anxiety, and what ends up happening.

Usually, when we feel anxious, we take action to get rid of that feeling or to resolve the situation that gave rise to it. And in many ways that is a sensible thing to do. If something feels bad, we seek to get rid of that, and to do so as quickly as possible. However, doing what we think will help us escape anxiety in the short-term can end up having the opposite effect in the longer-term. We are going to explore that pattern in much more detail in a later chapter.

BREAKING DOWN THE STORM

We are going to work toward helping you to support your loved one to make sense of anxiety in this way.

First of all, it is useful to select a specific example to work through to keep the process reasonably simple and manageable. Using a general situation like 'having an anxiety attack' risks the process getting overwhelmed with an overload of information, and multiple examples being tangled up together.

It is better to focus on a specific example and repeat with other examples. The more you repeat this process, the more clearly you will see themes and similarities emerge across each one.

When trying this out, ask the person you are supporting to choose an example that is:

- Recent
- Specific
- Not too distressing to focus on

The first factor we want to identify is the situation. You don't need to have lots of detail about the situation at this stage. You just need enough information to create an outline of what was going on. To get this information, you can ask the person to tell you:

- Where they were
- Who else was there
- What was going on right before they noticed their anxiety rise

Let's practise by looking at George's situation:

For George, an anxiety-provoking situation might be the moment when his wife Helen told him that they have been invited to an old friend's 60th birthday party, and that this will involve travel and an overnight stay.

So, if you were working through this situation with George, you might agree that the situation was as follows:

'Helen told me that we have been invited to a party and that we will have to stay overnight.'

Next, we want to identify what thoughts were triggered in the situation. To help the other person identify thoughts, you can ask questions like:

- What went through your mind in that moment?
- What did you think?
- How did you make sense of what was going on?
- If I could Bluetooth my headphones into your mind at that moment, what would I have heard?

In George's case, thoughts may have included:

- *'What if the car breaks down on the way there?'*
- *'What if we get a puncture? I might not manage to change the tyre. I might have a heart attack trying to change a tyre.'*
- *'What if something happens and one of the children needs us while we are away?'*
- *'Something might go wrong with the house while we are away.'*
- *'If something goes wrong, I will not be able to cope.'*

Following on from identifying thoughts, we consider what feelings occurred. Usually there is a clear link between the tone of the thoughts and the type of emotions that are triggered.

By looking at the thoughts that George experienced, we might expect him to feel emotions such as:

- *Anxiety*
- *Panic*
- *Fear*

Once these emotions are activated, our bodies become involved instantly. The physical experience is the *whoosh* of the fight-or-flight response.

For George, a number of physical changes occur as the situation unfolds. He might notice the following:

- *Heart beating faster*
- *Becoming hot and sweaty*
- *Struggling to think straight*

These factors combined influence how we behave: what we do, or do not do. When we experience difficult feelings, it is natural that we would act to escape how we feel. We might take steps to get out of the situation, or avoid entering a situation in the first place.

When we look at the thoughts that went through George's mind, and how he felt in his body, we understand why he would take action to lead him away from these unpleasant experiences. In this situation, George was keen to shut down plans, so that he could shut down anxiety.

Behaviour-wise George might:

- *Tell Helen that it does not sound like a good idea.*
- *Plan ways to get out of going.*
- *Walk away from the conversation.*

Broken down into the five components, George's experience can be understood like this:

George's initial thoughts focus on what could go wrong on the trip. That activates George's inner 'smoke detector' and the 'fire alarm' sounds. This means the fight-or-flight response is activated in the body, and George experiences anxiety, fear and panic.

The connection between thoughts, feelings and bodily sensations means that as George's physical and emotional anxiety rises, his negative thoughts snowball. He interprets his anxious response as meaning he can't cope, which feeds back into physical and emotional anxiety.

You can see how the feedback loops between each of the components of the anxiety storm interact rapidly to create an intense and distressing experience for George. The pattern escalates, generating a more intense feeling of panic, fear and anxiety, and strengthening the urge to escape.

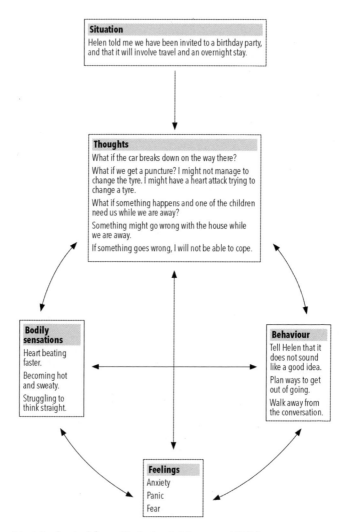

Situation
Helen told me we have been invited to a birthday party, and that it will involve travel and an overnight stay.

Thoughts
What if the car breaks down on the way there?

What if we get a puncture? I might not manage to change the tyre. I might have a heart attack trying to change a tyre.

What if something happens and one of the children need us while we are away?

Something might go wrong with the house while we are away.

If something goes wrong, I will not be able to cope.

Bodily sensations
Heart beating faster.

Becoming hot and sweaty.

Struggling to think straight.

Behaviour
Tell Helen that it does not sound like a good idea.

Plan ways to get out of going.

Walk away from the conversation.

Feelings
Anxiety
Panic
Fear

Model adapted from Padesky & Mooney, 1990[vii]

HOW TO HELP

- Use the five components diagram on page 64 to support your loved one to break down their experience of anxiety storms.
- Help the other person explore and clarify the difference between thoughts and feelings.
- Spend time looking at the ways in which the components feed into each other, causing anxiety to spiral.
- Together, work through a number of examples and see if you notice any themes.
- Remember, only progress to understanding once you have taken time to listen fully to the other person's experience.

SUMMARY

- The second step in the TURN method is UNDERSTANDING.
- We can improve our understanding of anxiety by breaking it down.
- The physical side of anxiety is an important part of the picture. The fight-or-flight response is designed to keep us safe, but sometimes it can feed into a pattern of anxiety and make us feel worse.

- We can break down an anxiety storm into five components. These are:
  - The situation
  - Thoughts
  - Feelings
  - The body
  - Behaviour
- These components interact and feed off each other, and this can cause anxiety to intensify quickly.
- You can help someone with anxiety by supporting them to break down their experience of anxiety in this way.

CHAPTER 5

PUTTING ANXIETY IN CONTEXT

We now know that there is an important difference between thoughts and feelings, but that they are closely linked and can feed back into each other to create a self-reinforcing loop. The strong link between thoughts and feelings is at the heart of anxiety storms.

How we feel in any situation is heavily influenced by what our interpretation of that situation has been. This is why, when we are supporting someone to understand their anxiety and make a change, we are interested in the thinking at the heart of their experience.

As we saw in the previous chapter, thinking plays a central and very influential role in shaping the experience of anxiety. Thinking patterns are also influential in keeping an emotional experience, such as anxiety, going. In other words, thoughts are a key player in the formation and escalation of anxiety storms.

REFRAMING AND REDIRECTING

The third step in the TURN method is made up of two parts: REFRAMING and REDIRECTING. First, we are going to look at reframing.

So, what do I mean by reframing? In the context of the TURN method, reframing relates to a change or shift in perspective. That might include gently changing the tone or focus of a thinking pattern, or altering the way in which something is interpreted. It can also mean reframing our relationship with thoughts more broadly. We will explore each of these options in this chapter.

I want to remind you again that it is important to follow the order of the TURN method as much as possible. If you can, make sure you give TIME to listen first (see Chapter 3). Second, it is important that you seek to help someone UNDERSTAND their experience of anxiety by breaking it down into its components (see Chapter 4)

Once you have done that, and you feel that a good connection and shared understanding has been established, it may be time to move on to look at the thinking patterns that show up as part of your loved one's experience of anxiety.

"Emotional struggles such as anxiety
are rarely triggered by one single factor,
but by the interaction of many factors
intertwined, and built up over time."

AN AWARENESS OF BACKGROUND FACTORS

When I see clients who want help with anxiety, we often spend time exploring their life history. This is because our life experience can shape how we make sense of the world in the here and now. Getting an understanding of how our background might influence our thinking processes in the present can be an empowering step to living better with anxiety.

The connection between early life experiences and present struggles can be complex. Emotional struggles such as anxiety are rarely triggered by one single factor, but by the interaction of many factors intertwined, and built up over time.

If someone's early life experiences have been traumatic, for example if they have survived abuse, neglect, repeated loss or other serious adversity, it may be that the influence on their mental and physical systems is beyond what can safely and realistically be addressed by the type of reframing we are going to cover in this book. If you suspect that this could be the case for the person you are supporting, or if they are able to confirm this to you, it may not be advisable to approach exploring past life experiences in your role as helper.

This is because the systems that we build to keep going after trauma can be important to us continuing to function and feeling safe. By exploring past traumas or seeking to reframe these, we can risk dismantling the coping strategies that keep the person going. This level of work should be done by a suitably qualified and experienced mental health professional (see Chapter 10).

Having said that, it can still be useful to have an understanding of some of the ways in which our background can shape our outlook. If nothing else, this knowledge can help us have empathy and compassion for ourselves and others at times where others' perspectives can be difficult to understand.

THE SAME IMAGE ON DIFFERENT BACKGROUNDS

For each of us, our perspective and world view grow out of our unique life experience and this influences the 'setting' on each of our inner smoke detectors. The background on which life's events are projected is different for all of us, which is why we all react differently to things. We all have deeply held beliefs and sensitivities that colour how we make sense of the world around us.

What affects one person one way can affect someone else totally differently. It doesn't mean either person is *wrong* or *less than* the other. It is just the effect of projecting the same image on to different backgrounds. The overall picture can end up looking completely different. We each have different truths, and everyone's truth is valid.

We are going to spend some time in this chapter looking at how certain types of beliefs can make us prone to making sense of life's events in a way that generates anxiety. Our deeply held beliefs set the background for how we interpret things in the here and now. Each of us might have a sensitivity to anxiety in relation to different triggers, depending on what our life experience and learning has been.

HOW TO HELP

- Be aware that anxiety may be related to events from early life, or more recent life events.
- Remember we each have an inner smoke detector, and its threshold is influenced by our life experience. Life events can alter the settings of the smoke detector at any time.
- Take caution around exploring the past with the person you are supporting, especially if they have survived traumatic experiences.

- Be aware of the limits to the help and support you can offer the other person if they have survived serious trauma or adversity. Of course, you can still be there for them, and you can apply the TURN method, but be cautious around challenging beliefs that may have an important protective factor.
- If the person you are helping indicates they would like to address issues to do with earlier life trauma, support them to explore ways in which they can access professional help for this.

THE ROLE OF UNCERTAINTY

We naturally have a preference for predictability and control. When things around us are ambiguous or unpredictable, our sense of threat tends to increase. When we face uncertainty, it is natural to feel threatened and anxious because our sense of security and predictability is undermined.

Control can be an important factor in feeling safe. When it seems as if our situation is overly ambiguous or out of control, we are likely to feel more vulnerable and more anxious.

When we find ourselves facing ambiguity, uncertainty or unpredictability, our threat response is more likely to be activated. A sense of not being in control can be interpreted as a sign of danger. If we have faced events in our early life where we felt particularly unsafe and out of control, we may be more prone to this kind of interpretation.

When we face ambiguous or unknown situations, some common thoughts might be:

- 'I am not in control.'
- 'I can't be safe if I am not in control.'
- 'I am powerless.'
- 'I am helpless.'

If you imagine yourself in a situation where any of these thoughts go through your mind, you can probably sense the anxiety that would occur.

THOUGHTS ABOUT HARM

As we know, the primary function of anxiety is to help keep us safe and away from danger. If we assess a situation as immediately threatening to our safety, our threat system activates right away, creating the experience of anxiety.

However, if we are prone to assessing situations as posing more of a threat than they actually do, our inner smoke detector may be more sensitive to indicators of this kind of threat in our environment.

If we have experienced physical harm or been unsafe in an earlier environment, then it makes sense that our inner smoke detector would be tuned in to threat of this nature. If in early life we learn that being attuned to threat of this kind has important survival value for us, then we will continue to use that approach as we move through life. Having faced illness or loss in early life can sometimes be connected to a tendency to interpret the world in this way.

This is not a conscious decision that we make; our system takes on this learning automatically. Again, this is our system's efforts to keep us safe.

If we are highly attuned to the possibility that we or someone close to us could come to harm, we may be more likely to detect signs of threat in our environment. That might mean we have a low tolerance for going into unknown situations, or leaving things to chance.

Some common thoughts around the theme of safety and harm are:

- 'I can't cope.'
- 'Something bad is going to happen to me.'
- 'I am going to be harmed.'
- 'I am going to die.'
- 'I am going mad.'
- 'Bad things happen when I least expect them.'

THOUGHTS ABOUT IDENTITY AND PERSONAL INTEGRITY

Sometimes, one of the most threatening appraisals we can make about a situation is that it carries negative meaning about who we are as a person. You have probably heard the term 'taking it personally'. That relates to the area of thoughts where we interpret a situation or outcome to mean something about our personal value, or our character.

Most of us would place importance on who we are as a person: it is natural for us to want to be an individual of worth; someone who makes a contribution and is able to be part of some form of community. It therefore makes sense that negative interpretations about our worth, ability, value or worthiness would trigger a threat response.

In my clinical experience, I have often observed that an early lack of encouragement, regard and attention, or the presence of excessive criticism, judgement and relentlessly high standards are some of the factors that can lead to a tendency to experience anxiety around personal value or integrity.

I have often noticed negative thoughts about self and identity in those who have survived prolonged humiliation or bullying, or who have faced being disbelieved.

If being judged negatively equated to threat in early life, then the inner smoke detector may be particularly attuned to situations where there is potential for being viewed negatively or 'getting it wrong'. Early life may have primed us to look out for the potential to be judged, and to keep ourselves safe from it.

Those who hold negative views of themselves can be more likely to interpret a situation as having negative meaning about them. This is one of the most common forms of anxious thoughts that I see in my therapy practice.

Some of the common thoughts around identity and personal integrity are:

- 'I am stupid.'
- 'I am a failure.'
- 'I am no good.'
- 'I am worthless.'
- 'I am not capable.'
- 'I am boring.'
- 'I am not as good/clever/attractive as everybody else.'
- 'Other people would dislike/ridicule/judge me if they knew the truth about me.'
- 'It is only a matter of time before everyone sees how stupid/incompetent/bad I really am.'

THOUGHTS ABOUT CONNECTION AND LOSS

As human beings, it is natural for us to want to have connections with others. Connection, community and relationships are important to us, and often provide the context for how we make sense of our lives.

It is also natural for us to want to have things that bring us joy, satisfaction, purpose, peace and hope. For many of us, these are the things that give life colour and meaning, and are a major driver for us in how we live our lives.

It is natural that we would feel a sense of threat if we interpreted any of those things to be in jeopardy.

Facing loss, inconsistency, separation or deprivation in early life relationships may make us more attuned to threat of future loss, rejection or separation.

Some thoughts I often hear around connection and loss are:

- 'Other people can't be trusted.'
- 'People always let me down eventually.'
- 'People always leave or die.'
- 'Things never work out for me.'
- 'It is dangerous to enjoy things because sooner or later it will all fall apart.'

OUR BELIEFS SHAPE OUR REALITY

In your experience of supporting someone who is living with anxiety, it is likely that there have been times when you have been tempted to tell them to just look at things differently. Perhaps you have heard yourself saying something like, 'It's not that bad' or 'Try not to look at it like that.'

Perhaps in your own anxious moments, you have had similar things said to you by well-meaning people.

> "Our lifelong attitudes and belief structures are deeply ingrained, and it can be extremely uncomfortable when we have to deal with information that goes against these structures."

When we recognize that a certain thought, belief system or attitude is not helping, wouldn't it be great if we could just choose to think something different? And yet, anyone who has been in the position of recognizing that a certain belief is not helpful knows that 'just change your mind' or 'just look at it another way' is usually not enough to make a difference.

If there is one thing that makes us uncomfortable above all else, it is when there is tension between what we believe, and the information we face in our environment. In other words, if we believe something, but are presented with evidence to the contrary, we feel uneasy. It is hard to sit with information that goes against what we believe.

Our lifelong attitudes and belief structures are deeply ingrained, and it can be extremely uncomfortable when we have to deal with information that goes against these structures.

Our minds are equipped with mechanisms that protect us from having to deal with this kind of dissonance. These mechanisms show up in our thinking, and influence how we make sense of and filter the information in our environment. This gives us an escape route from having to sit in the discomfort of facing evidence that challenges what we believe.

Our mind has two main strategies to get us out of this position:

- The first is to ignore, dismiss or minimize information that goes against what we believe.
- The second is to selectively attend to and focus on information that supports what we believe.

These mechanisms are especially powerful because they do not always operate at the conscious level. Without even thinking about it, we turn away from information that challenges our beliefs and turn our attention to evidence that supports our position. This fascinating process within our psychology is known as 'cognitive bias'.

COGNITIVE BIAS

When I talk to my clients about cognitive or thinking bias, I usually ask them which sports team they support. And if they are not into sports themselves, they can usually think of someone close to them who is.

If you ask a sports fan to tell you a bit about their team, you will probably find them to be pretty fluent in talking about the successes. They will reel off top scorers and defining moments of glory for as long as you are willing to listen.

If you ask them about losses, they may not offer up the same level of detail or enthusiasm. If they do talk about being beaten, they might talk about the injustice of what happened, the mitigating factors that were involved, and their unity with their team and fellow supporters in the aftermath of bitter defeat.

For many sports fans, the success of their own team might not be the subject in which they are most fluent. There is one other subject in which they may be even more knowledgeable. That is the defeats, failures and humiliations faced by their rival team.

This encyclopaedic knowledge is accounted for by more than just a love of the sport. This is cognitive bias in action.

Cognitive bias is the magic mirror that shapes information in our environment to fit with what we already believe.

Think about this from the perspective of the sports fan. You believe in your team. Therefore, you absorb the detail of your team's successes. You hold a strong and positive picture of your own team, supported by evidence of their greatness. You justify or nullify evidence that could call your team's greatness into question. You collect evidence of your team's superiority in relation to rivals. Why? To remain in the comfortable position of having a clear belief, undisturbed by doubt or question.

Bias influences how we make sense of information in our environment, and that is true for all of us. The tricky thing with bias is that it tends to be automatic, and to influence us without us being aware of its influence in the moment. So, if we are interested in changing a belief or perspective, recognizing bias can be an important place to start.

BIAS AND ANXIETY

Our thinking is biased toward information that supports our existing beliefs. Our beliefs about ourselves, others and the world in general shape our reality. These form the background on to which our day-to-day experiences are projected.

We are experts in distorting what is in front of us to fit our beliefs. This is not intentional; we often do it automatically, and without conscious awareness.

Let's take a look at how George's beliefs have influenced him:

During his career in the police force, George faced tragedy as a matter of routine. He was constantly exposed to the ways in which life can be dangerous and unfair. In his own life, George has seen how unexpected events can occur and change your life in an instant. Two of his close relatives died after short illnesses when George was growing up.

For George, keeping super-fit and maintaining high standards at work had been good ways of maintaining a sense of control. He was aware that he had a tendency to see the threat or risk in situations more than other people might, but was able to manage this because he felt confident in his own ability to handle things.

After retiring, George found that his sense of control gradually began to slip away. He started to fear that his body or mind could let him down, and noticed that he was becoming increasingly fearful around the potential for illness. He was also fearful that if something unexpected were to occur he would not be able to cope.

More and more, it seemed that things were going wrong in his day-to-day life. Matters like an appliance in the house breaking down, or his daughter having trouble with her car, started to occupy more space in George's mind. George found he focused more and more on things going wrong, and was less and less able to see his own ability to cope in these situations.

Considering George's life experience, it is possible that he might have developed beliefs about the world being unfair and dangerous. More recently, he may also have developed a view that he is not able to cope when things go wrong. This outlook might cause him to overestimate the likelihood of bad things happening in his own life, and to underestimate his ability to cope when things do go wrong.

Bias does two things, remember. It causes us to selectively tune in to evidence that supports what we believe, and to turn away from evidence that challenges what we believe.

For George, that could mean focusing on examples of when things have gone wrong and he has struggled. It could also mean not recognizing examples of when things have gone to plan and he has managed difficult situations well.

With Helen's support, George was able to see that he was prone to focusing on parts of life that fitted with his negative view. Together, they were able to recognize that uncertainty and a lack of control were significant for George. Through gentle exploration with Helen, George could notice his tendency to overanalyze signs of threat and risk in unknown situations. He could also see that there were times when he was able to cope perfectly.

THE POWER OF NOTICING

For some people, there might be a clear tendency to feel anxiety in relation to certain areas of life. And this might relate to the different areas of beliefs we looked at earlier.

In George's case, beliefs about control and about identity were particularly relevant.

It may be useful for you and the person you are supporting to get a shared sense of whether there is a noticeable theme that shows up in their thoughts when they are feeling particularly anxious. One way to do this is by exploring the themes covered in the chapter so far, and supporting the person you are helping to consider whether any of these resonate with them.

There may be no clear theme, but if you do detect one it can be a powerful observation, and it may direct how you go on to help the person you are supporting reframe some of their anxious thoughts.

In this process, there is something that is perhaps more important than whether or not you can help the person you are supporting identify a clear theme. When we start looking at thought processes, a subtle but important shift can take place. That is, we go from being consumed by a thought or pattern to being an observer of that thought or pattern.

For George, a conversation with Helen about the types of thoughts to which he was prone was useful not only because it allowed him to see a pattern and to make sense of that pattern in relation to his life experience, but also because it allowed him to step back a bit from his anxiety. George found that when he became an observer of his own patterns, they were somehow not quite so all-consuming.

For George, remembering he could choose to observe and reflect on his own experience in this way was an empowering reframe. By observing the storm, he found he was less likely to get caught up in the storm.

HOW TO HELP

- Once you have taken TIME and reached a shared UNDERSTANDING with the person you are supporting about their experience of anxiety, you can consider moving on to REFRAMING.

- In order to be able to reframe, support the person you are helping to explore the thinking patterns that make up part of their experience of anxiety.
- Use the five components model (see page 62) to break down recent anxiety storms, paying particular attention to the content of the thoughts that appear.
- With the person you are supporting, explore whether there could be a theme or themes to the thoughts that occur as part of anxiety storms. Noticing themes and recognizing their origins can provide new perspective. This has the potential to be empowering, and a reframe in its own right.
- If it feels right to do so, spend some time with the person you are supporting exploring the potential for bias in how they make sense of situations. Can they see a tendency to respond in line with their existing beliefs rather than evaluating each new situation in its own right?
- Be non-judgemental in your efforts to help your loved one identify any biases to which they may be susceptible.
- Be aware of the power of observing thoughts and thought patterns. By encouraging someone to look at their thoughts, you can help them take a step back from their thought patterns. This shift in perspective can be a powerful reframe.

SUMMARY

- The third step in the TURN method is REFRAMING and REDIRECTING.
- Reframing refers to shifting perspective in order to view things differently.
- Helping someone understand the context of their thoughts can be a powerful way of reframing.
- Early life experience, or more recent experience, can shape our belief system. This influences how we see ourselves, how we make sense of relationships with others and what we expect from the world in general. These underlying beliefs can shape how we make sense of situations in the here and now.
- Our interpretation of new situations is influenced by our existing beliefs. This means that we can unintentionally mould evidence in our environment to fit with what we believe, without being aware we are doing it.
- Supporting someone to get to know their beliefs and biases can be a powerful step toward shifting their perspective.
- When we observe thinking patterns, we step out of the experience and become an observer rather than a participant. Encouraging someone to observe their anxious thoughts can be a powerful way of helping them step out of the centre of an anxiety storm.

CHAPTER 6

REFRAMING ANXIOUS
THOUGHTS

Now that we have understood that context and background can influence how we make sense of things, let's move on to looking in more detail at how those influences can show up in the here and now.

When we face a situation that has any level of ambiguity or uncertainty, our brains like to fill the gaps for us, and they do that based on what we believe already.

Certainty, consistency and predictability appeal to us. And in the presence of ambiguity, bias can influence how we fill in the blanks. That means the more ambiguity or room for interpretation a situation holds, the more likely we are to distort it to fit with our existing beliefs and fears. The biases each of us carry make us susceptible to interpreting new or unclear situations in line with our existing beliefs.

Our mind's interpretation of what goes on around us is influenced by a collection of subtle thinking manoeuvres that we often make without realizing. Sometimes these are called cognitive distortions, or thinking errors.

These are cognitive mini-processes, little tricks of the mind, that filter information in order to fit with our existing beliefs. It is like looking in a magic mirror, where the reflection is what we want or expect to see, rather than exactly what is really there. These manoeuvres protect us from the discomfort of facing evidence that goes against what we believe. But in doing so, they can keep us stuck in a perspective that reinforces fear and anxiety.

COMMON THINKING MANOEUVRES IN ANXIETY

Cognitive Behavioural Therapy identifies a broad collection of thinking habits that can influence our perception, and therefore our emotions. Dr David Burns is a psychiatrist and researcher who has looked extensively at the role of cognitive distortions in shaping psychological patterns and experiences. Burns (1989) lists the ways in which our minds can distort information.[viii] In my experience, the following manoeuvres are some of the most common for those who experience anxiety:

Catastrophizing: Imagining or expecting the worst possible outcome for a situation before it has happened.

Mental filtering: Selectively pulling out small details of a situation and focusing on those without paying attention to the bigger picture.

All-or-nothing thinking: Categorizing information and experiences into all-or-nothing categories, such as good vs. bad, success vs. failure, or valuable vs. worthless.

Personalization: Interpreting situations or outcomes as being a reflection of who we are as a person.

Let's take a look at the role of thinking manoeuvres in shaping Catriona's experience of anxiety:

At school, Catriona was always at the top of her game. She never found it particularly difficult to consistently achieve top grades. She sometimes experienced a bit of anxiety during exams, but that was always transient and manageable.

When Catriona started university, she quickly found that being at the top of the class was not going to continue. She found the work challenging and fast-paced. She felt like it was a struggle to keep up – never mind excel – no matter how hard she worked or how diligently she studied. Despite passing all her assignments, and receiving top grades, Catriona experienced a dip in confidence. She began to doubt her own ability, and started contrasting her struggles with her fellow students, who seemed to be breezing through by comparison. The more she questioned her own ability, the more it seemed to her that she was not going to be able to cope with university.

Catriona found receiving feedback particularly difficult. Having never faced significant criticism of her work before, she took any negative comments or criticism as an indication that she was not smart enough to complete her degree.

As her negative view of herself took hold, she found critical feedback more and more devastating. Over time, Catriona felt engulfed by anxiety, and unable to function in exams as a result.

Let's look at some of the manoeuvres that Catriona's mind may have made:

1. Catastrophizing: Tutorials are often a trigger for Catriona. As she hears her fellow students talk and debate, she has thoughts about not being clever enough or good enough to be there. From there, she imagines failing all her exams, and being kicked out of university. She then imagines how she would explain this to her parents and extended family. She imagines watching her friends graduate as she sits out, having failed her degree. Catriona's anxiety spirals as she is pulled further and further into this mental narrative of the worst-case scenario.

2. Mental filter: Despite her grades and feedback being mostly positive, Catriona's mind focuses on any small negative comment in her feedback. Her mind filters out the abundance of positive evidence, meaning it does not get properly seen or recognized.

3. All-or-nothing thinking: Catriona sees only two possible outcomes for her studies, and for life in general: success or failure. This means that when she encounters challenges, her mind tells her she is not good enough to make a success of what she is trying to do, and that she is a failure. She categorizes her work, feedback and grades as either good or bad; there is no middle ground.

4. Personalization: When Catriona receives feedback that suggests areas for improvement in her work, she tends to take that as a personal criticism. In other words, she sees weakness or imperfection in her work as a reflection of weakness and imperfection in her as a person. Paired with all-or-nothing thinking, this means Catriona sees any imperfection in her work as an indication that she is a total failure as a person. If her work represents total failure, she herself must be a total failure.

HOW SMALL MANOEUVRES AFFECT THE BIGGER PICTURE

The advantage of thinking manoeuvres is that they protect us from having to confront information that goes against what we believe. Because of that, they protect us from the discomfort of cognitive dissonance.

But the longer-term cost of that can be problematic. It means that we do not always see evidence that goes against anxiety-provoking beliefs about ourselves, others and the world. We end up with a distorted view of reality. This is a self-fulfilling view, because we see what we believe and that then reinforces our beliefs.

In Catriona's case, we can see how her initial self-doubt triggers a confirmation bias that then distorts her reality. She focuses more and more on any evidence that supports her view of herself as a failure, and ignores, minimizes or discredits evidence to the contrary.

HOW TO HELP

- Begin with self-reflection. Going through the above section, did you recognize any of the thinking manoeuvres as applying to you?

- Notice what 'tricks' or manoeuvres your own mind uses to maintain your existing beliefs.
- Follow the TURN method to explore anxiety storms with the person you are supporting. Having broken the storms down into the five components (see page 62), work together to identify any thinking manoeuvres within the 'thoughts' component.
- Explore the role of thinking manoeuvres with the person you are supporting and, together, consider whether any show up consistently.
- Remember, sometimes recognizing and observing a pattern is a reframe in its own right.

RECAPPING THE REFRAMING PROCESSES

When I work with clients to identify bias, it often strikes me that getting an awareness of biases and thinking manoeuvres is, in itself, an important step toward change.

"Being able to observe thoughts rather than be consumed by them is a powerful way to step out of a spiralling anxiety storm."

Once someone has an awareness of their thinking styles, and some understanding of where they may have originated, it is easier to notice their influence in action.

There are three main processes within the REFRAMING stage:

- The first is gaining an understanding of the broader context of thinking styles. This is the part that involves considering how life experiences may have shaped our deeply held beliefs, and our outlook. Making these connections can be an important step in empowerment toward change.
- The second is noticing thinking patterns, styles and influences. This includes developing an awareness of bias and thinking manoeuvres, and observing how those influence anxiety storms. The better we are at noticing our thinking in the here and now, the more we are able to observe those influences when they show up. Being able to observe thoughts rather than be consumed by them is a powerful way to step out of a spiralling anxiety storm. Being able to notice thoughts also sets us up for the third process.
- The third process is consciously seeking to change thinking and see things from an alternative perspective. This is what we are going to focus on for the remainder of this chapter.

REDRESSING BALANCE

The thinking manoeuvres have one thing in common – they tend to root us in polar positions. It is all one thing or all something else. This style of thinking does not leave a lot of room for nuance or shades of grey.

Once you have supported the person with anxiety to identify and reflect on their biases and thinking manoeuvres, there are steps you can take to help them challenge those unhelpful thought patterns and work toward a more balanced and unbiased perspective. We are going to look at two approaches.

INTRODUCING SUPPORTIVE CHALLENGE

Perhaps the most obvious way of addressing a biased perspective is to call it out. This process involves supporting the other person to reality-test their thoughts, and challenge unhelpful or biased perspectives.

We have come far enough on this journey together for you to know the importance of doing this in a supportive way. If you were to jump to this way of helping without creating conditions of trust, respect and safety first, there is a strong chance that you could alienate the person you are seeking to help and leave them feeling criticized and misunderstood.

However, if you feel confident in your relationship with the other person, and have worked through the earlier steps in the

TURN framework, then you might consider introducing some supportive challenge.

'Thoughts are not facts': This has become a bit of a well-known saying in recent times, but I want to take a moment to break it down and think about what it actually means. It can be easy to forget that just because we *think* something does not necessarily mean it is true. We are often so caught up with our own thoughts that it does not occur to us to step back and question or challenge what our own mind is telling us.

> "Trying to ignore threat-related thoughts is unlikely to benefit anxiety, and could actually make the thoughts more dominant and difficult to escape over time."

Without even challenging a specific thought, the reminder that 'thoughts are not facts' can be an empowering reframe. This perspective can open up some flexibility in thinking, which in turn can lead to changes in anxiety.

It is important to be clear that this is not the same as saying 'thoughts are not facts, therefore just try to ignore them'. Trying to ignore threat-related thoughts is unlikely to benefit anxiety, and could actually make the thoughts more dominant and difficult to escape over time.

However, awareness that thoughts are not facts is an important gateway to questioning and challenging thoughts. That can lead to achieving a more balanced perspective, which is a key step to living better with anxiety.

Working with evidence: When you and the person you are supporting recognize that a particular thought may be biased or imbalanced, you can work together to challenge the thought using conscious reasoning. As part of this, you can look at the role of evidence. Factual evidence is the antidote to bias and assumptions. When we deal with evidence, we move away from bias, assumptions and supposition, and toward a perspective based in reality.

"This process is not about trying to convince the person experiencing anxiety to 'think positively' or trying to put an overly positive spin on a bad or difficult situation."

With the person you are supporting, first consider the evidence that supports the anxious thought. It is important to acknowledge evidence on both sides, so make sure you encourage them to share evidence that supports their existing perspective.

Following that, you can explore whether there may be evidence that does *not* support the thought. Bear in mind this can be a challenging process for the other person, because you are asking them to sit with information that goes against what they believe. We all find this uncomfortable!

Let's look at how Catriona's parents helped her to address some of her thinking manoeuvres:

With the help of her parents, Catriona was able to look objectively at the types of thoughts that came up for her when she was preparing for an exam. By breaking down her anxiety storm using the five components model, Catriona identified one particular thought that was recurring across anxiety storms. That thought was:

'I am going to fail.'

When looking at this thought together, Robert and Angela encouraged Catriona to see that, while she may have this thought in the moment, it is not necessarily true.

From there, they were able to work together to consider whether any thinking manoeuvres could be at play. Going through them one-by-one, they agreed that looking at things in terms of 'failure' versus 'success' was an all-or-nothing perspective. They also saw that jumping to the conclusion 'I am going to fail' was catastrophizing.

Catriona noticed that observing her thinking in this way allowed her to step back from the situation a bit.

She agreed to explore the evidence for and against the thought, with her parents.

First, they explored evidence in support of the thoughts. Catriona quickly came up with evidence such as:

- *'I am not as clever as some other people on my course.'*
- *'I sometimes get feedback that I need to improve parts of my work.'*
- *'I have to put in a lot of time and hard work to keep up.'*

They then moved on to considering evidence that would not support the thought, 'I am going to fail.' With help from Robert and Angela, Catriona recognized that the following evidence was true:

- *'I am on a difficult course, and hard work is to be expected.'*
- *'One piece of criticism does not mean my work is poor overall.'*
- *'I have passed every exam and piece of coursework to date.'*
- *'I have received positive as well as negative feedback.'*

This process is not about trying to convince the person experiencing anxiety to 'think positively' or trying to put an overly positive spin on a bad or difficult situation. The aim is to address the anxiety-enhancing effects of bias by helping the person make a logical and reasoned assessment of the day-to-day situations they face.

If you can support the person you want to help to reduce the role of bias, you can, in turn, help them take a step toward better managing anxiety.

SEEING THROUGH SOMEONE ELSE'S EYES

When I am working with clients on reframing, I find that one of the most powerful ways to gain a quick shift in perspective is to ask the person how a supportive friend or relative might view the situation.

Sometimes, when we try to assess evidence from our own perspective, our beliefs and biases can make it difficult to see evidence that does not support our fear.

However, by stepping into someone else's shoes, we can see the situation in a more balanced and reasoned way.

This is something Robert and Angela supported Catriona to do:

When Catriona looked at her experience at university, all she could see was the struggles, the negative feedback and the comparisons with other students who seemed to have it all under control.

Catriona's parents asked her to consider how someone else close to her might view how she was getting on. They encouraged Catriona to think about how her closest childhood friend might see her.

From this stance, Catriona was able to see that getting on to her course, at her university, was in itself a massive achievement. She was also able to see that other parts of who she was – such as her fun-loving nature and her loyalty as a friend – made up important parts of her character.

By viewing herself through the eyes of a friend, Catriona was able to broaden her perspective. This let her see a fuller picture, challenging the limited view caused by biased thinking.

HOW REFRAMING AFFECTS ANXIETY

When you support someone to recognize that their thoughts are not facts, and to shift or broaden their perspective, you assist them to reframe the way in which they make sense of their experience.

The link between thinking and emotions is at the centre of this change. Altering how we make sense of something is a gateway to changing emotional experience. This is why REFRAMING is such an important step in the TURN model.

Let's look at how this helped Catriona:

For Catriona, working through the evidence this way with the support of her parents, allowed her to address some of the bias in her thinking and see the situation more clearly. She was able to recognize that, while finding academic work challenging was new for her, she was able to cope.

Similarly, challenging herself to consider how her situation might be interpreted by someone else let her reframe her thinking.

These techniques for shifting perspective made a difference to Catriona's anxiety. She was more able to take a balanced view when facing difficult feedback, and this meant that her confidence was not negatively affected as it had been before. By continuing to challenge her thinking bias, Catriona was able to interrupt the self-fulfilling loop of negative thoughts.

HOW TO HELP

- Before challenging thoughts, make sure you have fully listened to the person you are helping, and have validated their experience.
- Sensitively highlight that thoughts are not necessarily facts; our interpretations and reactions are often coloured by pre-existing beliefs.

- With the person's consent, explore together how you could challenge some of the thoughts that show up in anxiety storms.
- Help the person identify evidence that supports their initial perspective, and then to consider evidence that may support an alternative perspective.
- Encourage them to see the situation through the eyes of a supportive friend, and to consider what that person's perspective might be.

SUMMARY

- Our minds use subtle manoeuvres to make what we see fit with what we already believe.
- Noticing the manoeuvres the mind makes is an important step toward managing anxiety.
- Noticing patterns and tendencies is an important reframe in its own right.
- We can address confirmation bias by challenging thoughts.
- Exploring evidence is one way of challenging thoughts.
- Assuming the position of a supportive friend can help us see things from a different perspective.

CHAPTER 7

THE ROLE OF BEHAVIOUR

In the TURN framework, R stands for REFRAMING, which we covered in the previous chapter, and REDIRECTING, which relates to the ways in which behaviour can influence the experience of anxiety. In this chapter, we are going to see how behaviours can often be the component that feeds anxiety and keeps it going, and explore ways to help redirect certain behaviours, in order to break the cycle of anxiety.

Before she was unwell, a typical week for Mishka involved a busy and unpredictable work schedule. She would go for a couple of runs and to the gym, and see friends for drinks, the cinema and gigs. At the weekend, she would often participate in outdoor sports, and enjoy going out for meals or visiting family.

Since being unwell, the prospect of being out and about feels overwhelming for Mishka. She has planned to see friends or to go for a trip to the countryside with her partner and the dogs, but cancelled at the last minute. Even when Mishka thinks about going out, she notices her breathing becoming shallower, her mouth becoming dry, and her palms becoming sweaty. When this starts to get overwhelming, Mishka cancels her plans.

Mishka now prefers to stay at home in a familiar environment, where she doesn't have to experience these unpleasant feelings. She has had a friend round for coffee now and then, but even that causes anxiety.

Mishka's partner, Emma, just wants Mishka to feel better. She hates to see her upset and fearful, and does whatever she can to make her feel safe. Emma misses their former life, but her priority is looking after Mishka in whatever way she can.

Mishka and Emma's close friends miss seeing them but, after repeated cancellations, are beginning to think their invitations are not wanted. They have backed off calling and visiting because they don't want to make life more difficult for the couple.

HOW THE STORM BECOMES A HURRICANE

Because behaviour tends to be visible, it is often the part of anxiety that is most noticeable from the outside. A change in your loved one's behaviour may well have been the first thing that alerted you to their difficulties. It may have been that you saw changes appear gradually and that, looking back, you can see these changes were caused by their efforts to manage their anxiety over time.

"Someone living with anxiety may withdraw from and avoid things they used to do effortlessly. This can be a sad and painful change to witness."

Anxiety may have its origins in the body and mind, but behaviour is often what escalates and prolongs the experience.

By behaviour, we mean actions. We mean what we *do*. But we also mean what we do *not* do. This is important to remember.

When anxiety strikes, our instinct is often to do less. In practical terms, that means the person living with anxiety is likely to withdraw from and avoid things they used to do effortlessly. As someone looking on, this can be a sad and painful change to witness.

THE SWEET RELIEF OF AVOIDANCE

In many ways, we are simple creatures. When we like something, we want more of it. And when we find a certain action is likely to get us more of what we like, we do more of that action.

Similarly, if we do not like something, and we find that a certain action is likely to get us more of what we don't like, we do less of that action. Or we try to cut it out altogether. Why wouldn't we? No one wants to feel bad.

As a life strategy, it's not a bad one. Do more of what brings you what you like, and less of what brings you what you don't like. For example, a child who touches a hot cooker links the pain in their fingers with touching the cooker, because the pain occurs instantly. A child who receives a chocolate button as a reward for good table manners links the chocolate button with the table manners because the two things occur close together.

In psychology, this is called conditioning, and it is when two things occur close together and we learn to associate them, and to respond similarly through association.

Timing is essential to this kind of learning. For us to associate a behaviour with a certain outcome, the two things need to occur close together in time. To take the above example, if the sore hand came the day after touching the cooker, the child would not associate the outcome with the behaviour. If the chocolate button came a week after, the child would not associate it as a reward for the good table manners.

As a strategy for anxiety, avoidance delivers fast. With the *whoosh* underway in the body, and the mind focused on negative possibilities and bad outcomes, it makes sense that we would look for an escape route. If we come to associate certain situations, events or people with the feelings of anxiety, it is natural for us to pull away from these things.

If something makes us feel bad we want less of it. If the *whoosh* is the instant outcome in certain situations, we associate the *whoosh* with those situations, and seek to avoid them in future.

Let's look at how this played out for Mishka:

It is understandable that, for Mishka, the prospect of engaging with parts of her old life after a period of illness could feel anxiety-provoking. Even the prospect of seeing friends or family sets off the 'whoosh' in her body, and triggers a trail of thinking about all the things that could go wrong.

As we know, the anxiety storm escalates as thoughts and feelings interact. For Mishka, thoughts about not being able to cope cause her inner smoke detector to keep signalling, leading to her feeling out of breath, hot, sweaty and fuzzy in her mind. Her mind then notices that, and tells her she is unwell again, and that she definitely would not cope with going out. And so the anxiety storm continues to build.

Who wouldn't want an escape route out of such a difficult experience? When Mishka makes the simple decision 'I am not going', the physical 'whoosh' of anxiety subsides almost immediately, and is replaced with the welcome 'aaaah' of relief.

And of course, when something makes us feel good or feel better, we quickly learn to do more of it. So, for Mishka, planning to go out to see friends feels bad; deciding to stay at home feels good. The more Mishka makes that association, the more she learns that staying in and saying no to plans is what feels good and safe. Over time, avoiding anxiety-provoking situations becomes a default strategy for Mishka. The more she avoids, the more difficult it becomes to break the cycle and make her way back to her old life.

I FEEL BETTER – WHAT'S THE PROBLEM?

If we associate getting away from the source of anxiety with the *aaaah* of relief, it makes sense that we would repeat that whenever the fire alarm starts to sound.

You may have seen this clearly with the person you are supporting. You may even know the feeling yourself. For example, think about being invited to a social event that you really don't want to attend, but where you need to put in an appearance. When you think about it, your threat system activates, and you feel the *whoosh*. Your mind comes up with negative predictions about what the event will be like, including the people you don't want to spend time with, and how you will feel out of place, bored and uneasy. The feeling intensifies as the date comes closer. On the day, you receive a message that the event has been cancelled. *Aaaah.*

Relief is a powerful reward. And powerful rewards make us more likely to repeat the behaviour that brought that reward around. Like the chocolate button: it is delivered instantly, so we link it with what has just gone before.

"Avoidance is a natural go-to response when we experience anxiety."

For those living with anxiety, the wash of relief that comes with getting away from anxiety-provoking situations can seem irresistible. The *aaaah* is instant, so we learn to associate avoiding the situation with the relief of feeling good.

Let's go back to Mishka:

Prior to her illness, Mishka lived a busy and active life, and rarely struggled with anxiety. As a naturally outgoing person, she loved spending time with others, and going into new environments. And, of course, the more she did and enjoyed, the more she wanted to do.

When she was unwell, Mishka was not able to work, socialize and exercise in the way she used to. The positive association between her activities and positive feelings faded during her illness. And now the thought of re-entering her old life makes Mishka feel apprehensive and anxious.

When an invitation comes from friends to meet for lunch, Mishka immediately feels the 'whoosh' of anxiety. Thoughts going through her mind include:

- *'I won't be able to cope.'*
- *'I will feel out of place.'*
- *'I will be overwhelmed by people's conversations and questions.'*
- *'What if I feel unwell while we are out?'*
- *'I can't face being in a busy and crowded place.'*

Mishka's threat system is activated right away, and continues to be activated every time she thinks ahead to the lunch.

The day before the lunch is due to happen, Mishka feels overwhelmed with anxiety. When the anxiety storm reaches its peak, Mishka decides to text her friends and tell them she won't be able to make it. 'Aaaah!' The anxiety storm subsides instantly.

While Emma is disappointed that the lunch will not be going ahead, she supports Mishka's decision to cancel it. After all, if it was making Mishka's anxiety worse, it was not worth it.

Avoidance is a natural go-to response when we experience anxiety. It makes sense in the moment, creates an instant sense of safety and delivers the *aaaah* of relief from being out of the threatening situation.

Some examples of avoidance that I often see in my clinical work include:

- Cancelling plans (such as social events, holidays, meetings or work commitments) at the last minute because of fear about how it will go.
- Avoiding medical appointments or health checks due to fearing embarrassment or a bad outcome.
- Staying in the same job/house/relationship when unhappy because of anxiety about making a change.
- Turning down opportunities because of fear of not being good enough.
- Avoiding going to the shops/school gates/social events for fear of not knowing what to say in conversations.
- Keeping super-busy in order to avoid thinking about or doing what causes anxiety.

It may be that you can recognize some of these examples in the behaviour of the person you are supporting, and it may be impacting you – you may be living with limits placed on your life and your activities.

In my work, I often see the effects of avoidance not just on the person living with anxiety, but on those close to the person. I want to acknowledge the potential impact of that on you, including the sacrifice and disappointment that can be part of the reality of being close to someone who lives with anxiety. In Chapter 11, we will explore how you can take steps to care for yourself in relation to this.

THE COST OF AVOIDANCE

You can probably think of times in your own life when you have dealt with anxiety through avoidance. We all do it. And doing that now and again can be a reasonable way of dealing with anxiety. But if we do it repeatedly, and with situations that are important, three things happen. Consider whether you have noticed any of the following occur for the person you are supporting:

1. Missing out on the important things: Connections with friends and family, and our ability to do the activities that add colour to our lives, begin to fade. The longer we continue with avoidance as a strategy, the more we will lose over time. As a result, our lives will become smaller and smaller.

2. The anxiety-controlling behaviour becomes problematic:
The behaviour we adopt to try to control our anxiety ends up becoming a bigger problem than the anxiety itself.

Often, when clients initially come to me for therapy, it is because they have reached the stage where the behaviours they have been using to try to manage difficult feelings like anxiety have started taking over their lives. For someone experiencing anxiety, it may be that certain behaviours helped them manage anxiety up to a point, but that these behaviours have gradually become more limiting over time.

It might be that by avoiding meeting new people they now feel lost and alone, while longing for a relationship. It might be that what started off as missing a few classes at university because they did not feel on top of the work has become missing several months' teaching, and feeling overwhelmed, panicky and hopeless about facing the consequences. Such avoidance behaviours may well have been what first alerted you that the person you are seeking to help was experiencing anxiety.

When we find ourselves behaving in ways that we recognize as holding us back, or making us feel trapped and unhappy, and ask ourselves why, the answer is often this: we do it because there was a time when it helped us avoid feeling anxious or uncomfortable, and when it helped us feel safe and in control.

Sometimes clients who are struggling with anxiety tell me they worry they are crazy, out of control or beyond help because of the behavioural cycles they have ended up locked in. But what we must remember is that these cycles are driven by our basic desire to get away from bad feelings. It doesn't make us crazy, but it can indicate we need to update our settings.

3. We miss out on the opportunity to disprove our negative predictions: In the moment, we do not associate avoidance with negative outcomes. Why not? Because the negative outcome does not occur right away. Think back to the child and the hot cooker (see page 118). If the sore hand occurred a week after touching the cooker, the association between the two things would not be formed.

"Be aware that you could be feeding in to avoidance, with the best of intentions."

Remember, learning by association depends on timing. The short-term outcome of avoidance is sweet relief. Because the cost of avoidance is not instantly apparent, we do not learn to associate avoidance and loss so easily. That tends to be a slower realization, which emerges gradually over time.

As a supporter of someone who experiences anxiety, you will already know that, ultimately, loss can be the biggest cost. Anxiety itself is not the most limiting factor. It is the things we do (or the things we avoid) to try to control our anxiety that cost us most dearly in the long-term. Over time we can become locked into a pattern of avoidance, which gradually dismantles the parts of life that matter most to us – the connections, the opportunities, the moments of vitality – until we are left with very little but our fear.

HOW TO HELP

- Remember, avoidance may well have worked as a coping strategy at an earlier point in life. It is not *wrong*, but it may be *out of date*.
- Be aware that avoidance may look like it helps with anxiety in the here and now, but remember that the short-term relief is often outweighed by long-term cost.
- Take time to support your loved one to identify their go-to avoidance strategies.
- Gently support them to reflect on what avoidance has cost them.
- Be aware that you could be feeding in to avoidance, with the best of intentions. Can you identify times when you have encouraged avoidance because you just wanted the other person to feel better in that moment?
- Be prepared to challenge your own role in colluding with avoidance.
- Be prepared to gently challenge your loved one when you recognize avoidance being used as a strategy to manage anxiety.

USING BEHAVIOUR TO FEEL SAFE

George likes to know where his family members are and what they are doing, as this helps him to feel more in control, and less anxious. When his wife goes out, he likes her to call or text when she arrives at her destination, and to let him know when she is heading home. He will often call her once or twice while she is out to check she is OK. George doesn't leave the house when his wife is out, in case something happens and he misses a call on the landline to tell him about it.

George calls his adult children a number of times a day to check in on them. While they like hearing from their dad, sometimes they will go to their phone to see several missed calls and some messages from him. This can cause anxiety for them, and they feel pressure to keep him informed about their movements constantly, so that his anxiety does not get worse. George finds it comforting to receive regular updates because it assures him that everyone is safe.

George finds it highly anxiety-provoking when his wife, son or daughter go on a long journey, particularly in the car. When this happens, George sometimes checks the news and social media to check for word of accidents.

On one occasion, George's daughter was stuck in traffic and her phone ran out of battery. George's anxiety escalated to the point that he began phoning round hospitals to see if a woman matching his daughter's description had been admitted to the Emergency Department. By the time George's daughter could reassure him she was OK, George was highly distressed and convinced the worst had happened.

One of the main triggers for anxiety storms can be ambiguity, or a lack of complete information. Nature hates a vacuum; when we have incomplete information, our mind seeks to fill the gaps. When we live with anxiety, we are likely to fill those gaps by imagining the worst possible scenarios and outcomes. As we saw in the previous chapter, our existing biases influence how we make sense of that ambiguity.

When getting out of a situation by using avoidance is not an option, another route to the *aaaah* of relief can be to double down on behaviours that increase our sense of being in control.

Often, we use behaviour in this way when we face ambiguity, or a lack of control. If we can't avoid the situation altogether, we will use other ways to fill gaps in information or reduce ambiguity.

For George, this means contacting family members frequently, checking news, and generally trying to have as much information as possible to feel more in control and keep anxiety at bay.

Behaviours used in this way are sometimes called 'safety behaviours'. This is a bit of a misleading term because it implies that these behaviours keep us safe. In fact, what they do is help us *feel* safe, by giving us a sense of being in control. But, like avoidance, the use of safety behaviour can keep us stuck in a cycle of anxiety.

Some examples of safety behaviours that I see in my clinical work, and that you might recognize in the person you are supporting, include:

- Seeking reassurance from loved ones or others that they are safe/happy/that everything is OK.
- Being constantly on the look out for any physical changes or symptoms, and spending extensive lengths of time Googling health concerns.
- Constantly scanning the environment looking for any sign of danger or threat.
- Constantly checking the news or social media.
- Striving to maintain extremely high standards (for example in work, relationships, domestic cleanliness or productivity) in order to avoid rejection, failure or humiliation.
- Explaining things at considerable length and in detail to make sure no detail is ever left out, and to minimize room for ambiguity or error.
- Scrutinizing people's words and expressions for signs of disapproval in conversation.
- Keeping a low profile by staying silent or keeping out of the way to avoid negative judgements or criticism.

THE PROBLEM WITH SAFETY BEHAVIOURS

The irony of safety behaviours is that they can often end up having the opposite to the desired effect.

Let's go back to George.

George relies on checking news and social media when he is anxious about his family members' safety. When he does this, he looks specifically for news of road accidents. This means that he ends up spending a lot of time reading about road accidents. While he gets some reassurance in the short-term when he realizes that his family members could not have been involved, this practice only makes him more anxious about safety in the longer-term because he is disproportionately exposed to bad news about road safety.

Another of George's safety behaviours is checking on his family members regularly to seek reassurance from them. George's wife and children only want him to feel better. They hate seeing him afraid and distressed, so they respond by being available as much as possible, and providing the reassurance George seeks so he can set his mind at ease. This gives George relief in the short-term, but ultimately does not help his anxiety.

Like avoidance, safety behaviours can make anxiety more manageable in the short-term. However, the more they are used, the more the person gets locked in a pattern where they depend on safety behaviours in order to cope. And, ironically, safety behaviours can feed the anxiety, adding to the person's difficulties in the long-term.

HOW TO HELP

- Remember that, like avoidance, safety behaviours may well have worked as a coping strategy at an earlier point in someone's life. They are not *wrong*, but they may be *out of date*.
- Be aware that using safety behaviours can look like they help the person you are supporting in the here and now, but the short-term relief is often outweighed by the long-term cost.
- Take time to support the person to identify their go-to safety behaviour.
- Be aware that you could be feeding in to safety behaviours, with the best of intentions. Are there times when you provide reassurance or get involved with other safety behaviours because you want to reduce your loved one's anxiety in the short-term?
- Be prepared to challenge your own role in colluding with their safety behaviours.
- Be prepared to gently challenge the person you are supporting when you recognize safety behaviours being used as a strategy to manage anxiety.

"Be prepared to gently challenge your loved one when you recognize safety behaviours being used as a strategy to manage anxiety."

And, like avoidance, using safety behaviours means the person misses out on the chance to learn that they can be safe without the behaviour. In other words, they don't get the chance to disprove their negative predictions about what will happen if they drop their safety behaviours.

YOUR ROLE IN AVOIDANCE

We have looked at how those living with anxiety can use avoidance and safety behaviours to try to manage anxiety, and how this can often make things worse in the longer-term, because these behaviours feed into the pattern that keeps anxiety going.

As a supporter of a person living with anxiety, this pattern might be the trickiest thing of all to manage well. You hate seeing your loved one suffer. All you want is for them to feel better.

In the short-term, buying into avoidance and safety behaviours can ease anxiety for the person you are supporting.

It is completely natural and understandable that you may have found yourself encouraging avoidance, or enabling safety behaviours.

Since her illness, Mishka has felt increasingly anxious about reintegrating back into her old life. She has managed this by cutting off anxiety-provoking situations as much as she can. When social events have come up, the 'whoosh' of anxiety has felt unbearable, so she has opted out, and enjoyed the sweet relief of avoidance. Over time, this approach has not only kept Mishka's anxiety going, but caused her life to shrink and her friends to start keeping their distance.

Until now, Emma, has supported Mishka when she has avoided social contact or other activities. Emma can see that the thought of such things cause a spike in Mishka's anxiety. Emma's intentions around enabling Mishka's avoidance are completely well-meaning and positive. But unfortunately, by encouraging Mishka to cancel and to steer away from what makes her anxious, Emma has ended up colluding with avoidance and strengthening a pattern that feeds Mishka's anxiety.

However, the best approach would *not* be to completely cut out *any* avoidance or *all* safety behaviours. When someone depends on these behavioural strategies to cope (and we all do to varying extents!), it would be cruel and unhelpful to seek to remove them suddenly, and in the name of helping.

You can imagine what might happen if Emma decided that enough was enough and invited ten friends round for a dinner party and forced Mishka to go through with it. Not only could this be distressing and overwhelming for Mishka, but it could break down trust between her and Emma irreparably.

So, if avoidance and safety behaviours can feed into anxiety, but stripping these strategies away in one go is not the best approach, how do we move forward?

The answer to that is: one step at a time, and always with consent.

THE GRADED APPROACH

Having looked at how avoidance and safety behaviours feed in to anxiety, we know that these strategies are not the answer to managing anxiety in the long-term.

Ultimately, holding on to avoidance and safety behaviours keeps anxiety going, and stops the person living with anxiety from discovering that they can be OK without them.

"The key to letting go of avoidance and safety behaviours is to redirect gradually, and with the person living with anxiety holding the reins."

The answer is not to bulldoze these behaviours! I don't think any of us would appreciate someone else boldly pointing out the little things each of us does to feel safe or achieve momentary relief from discomfort, and then whipping them away like a carpet from under us.

When we think about redirecting avoidance and safety behaviours, it is essential that we proceed gently, and with care.

The key to letting go of avoidance and safety behaviours is to redirect gradually, and with the person living with anxiety holding the reins.

In CBT, we use an approach called 'graded exposure'. This recognizes that holding on to avoidance and safety behaviours keeps anxiety going, but also that it would be overwhelming and probably unwise to aim to stop these behaviours all at once, because they provide what feels like a life raft in a sea of anxiety.

The process of letting go of avoidance and safety behaviours is a gradual one. Like climbing a long flight of stairs, the way to do it is to take one step at a time. The aim is to support the person you are supporting to gradually build their tolerance, as they let go of avoidance and safety behaviours bit by bit.

Of course, letting go of a safety behaviour initially will mean that the *whoosh* of anxiety occurs with gusto, and that will take time to subside. I tell my clients that this space – where the *whoosh* takes hold but they resist the urge to avoid or use a safety behaviour – is the space where they will make real progress toward living better with anxiety.

The process is about gradually growing tolerance for the *whoosh*, so that the physical feelings of anxiety become more and more bearable with every step. As our tolerance to the *whoosh* increases, we become able to do a bit more, so tolerance increases again, and we can do more. This process continues until, eventually, the person living with anxiety can achieve the task at the top of the staircase.

They may well continue to feel anxiety as they complete the tasks, but their tolerance for that anxiety will increase with every step.

CONSTRUCTING A STAIRCASE

Let's take a look at how a graded approach worked for Mishka…

Working together, Mishka and Emma came up with a ten-step exposure 'staircase'.

At the very top of the staircase was the task that Mishka most wanted to achieve, but that felt almost unachievable at the start. For her, that was to have a weekend away with Emma and some of their closest friends, which included doing a sporting activity during the day, staying in a hotel, and enjoying a meal and drinks in the hotel restaurant.

It is essential that the steps on the staircase have meaning. They need to tie in with where the person ultimately wants to get to with their anxiety. Remember, it is not necessarily about getting rid of anxiety, but about building a tolerance to what can be done in the presence of anxiety.

For Mishka, her relationship with Emma, their friendships, and an active social and outdoor life were some of the most important parts of her life. She longed to be able to take part in fun activities like they used to. For her, being able to go on that sort of trip again would represent her being able to live well with anxiety.

At the mid-point of the ladder was a challenging but more achievable task – for Mishka to go the gym and attend a class on her own for an hour. Again, this ties in with Mishka's personal values around fitness and having an active life.

The lower levels of the staircase were made up of tasks that felt immediately more manageable, though still challenging, for Mishka.

Mishka's Exposure Staircase

1. Go with Emma to get a takeout coffee.
2. Take the dogs for a walk in the local park with Emma at a quiet time of day.
3. Go to the coffee shop with Emma and sit in this time.
4. Drive to the supermarket alone and buy a few items.
5. Go to the gym alone and participate in a class.
6. Take the dogs for a walk in the local park alone at a busy time of day.
7. Go out for a meal with Emma and two closest friends in a busy restaurant.
8. Go into the office to see her manager and other co-workers.
9. Have a whole day out with Emma and a number of friends in the countryside.
10. Go away for the weekend with Emma and a number of friends including staying in a hotel, having a meal and drinks in the hotel restaurant, and participating in an outdoor activity.

When I work with my clients to put together an exposure staircase, I encourage them to think of it as being a bit like a training programme.

Like any good training programme, each step should feel manageable because it builds on what was achieved in the previous step.

Approaching this piece of work is like approaching going up a big flight of stairs: if you look right up to the top at the beginning, the task can feel insurmountable. But if you focus just on the first step and keep going, one by one, you will eventually look back down and be amazed how far you have been able to climb.

When working through an exposure staircase, we are gradually building tolerance to anxiety, through exposure. It works because, with every step, the person becomes more and more able to tolerate the anxiety involved with doing each task. And with that, their confidence grows and they feel able to take another step.

'SITTING OUT' THE WHOOSH

Working through an anxiety staircase can be a demanding challenge. In approaching this, the person you are supporting is going to be opening the door to the *whoosh* of anxiety. Understandably the temptation to manage that with safety behaviours is likely to show up.

When working through an exposure staircase with my clients, I always look out for signs of safety behaviours. And as we get toward the more challenging end of the staircase, safety behaviours become more and more likely to put in an appearance.

Let's look at Mishka's experience of working through the exposure staircase:

For Mishka, the first few levels of the staircase felt fairly manageable. From levels 1 to 3, she was accompanied by Emma, which was an important part of feeling safe. She noticed the 'whoosh' of anxiety every time, but was able to manage that and get through the task.

Levels 4, 5 and 6 involved Mishka completing tasks on her own, without Emma. When she was doing these tasks, she found that she had a strong urge to be in touch with Emma while she went about her task. When driving to the supermarket, Mishka was tempted to be on the phone to Emma on loudspeaker the entire time. However, between them, Mishka and Emma recognized that this would be a safety behaviour, which could undermine the progress of Mishka's hard work.

There may be a temptation to manage the anxiety by using safety behaviours, but this can interfere with the success of this approach because they get in the way of the person feeling the anxiety, and building their tolerance to it with each step.

"Small increments tackled successfully are better than overly ambitious leaps that set the person up to struggle."

Sometimes, someone progressing through an exposure staircase might get stuck at a certain level where they do not yet feel able to tackle the next task. This is usually a sign that that task perhaps belongs further up the staircase than it is currently positioned. If this happens, you can support the person you are helping to consider re-positioning that task, and to come up with new, more manageable, tasks that can be tackled successfully, at their current level.

There may be some trial and error involved in finding the right tasks for the right levels of the staircase. Remember, each task should build on the last. Tasks should be challenging, but ultimately manageable. There is no limit to the number of steps the staircase can have. Small increments tackled successfully are better than overly ambitious leaps that set the person up to struggle.

THE *WHOOSH* DOESN'T LAST FOREVER

When our threat system is activated, and the inner smoke detector goes off, the *whoosh* of anxiety is rapid and intense.

In the early moments of the *whoosh*, it can feel like the physical feelings are going to keep escalating until the experience becomes completely intolerable. It is usually this sensation that causes us to reach for avoidance and safety behaviours. When our body feels out of control, it is completely natural to want to intervene and return it to normal as quickly as possible. The *aaaah* of relief is all we want.

But when we interrupt the *whoosh* by using a behaviour to regulate our feelings, two things happen:

1. The *aaaah* of relief occurs, but our state of relief is usually short-lived.
2. We miss out on discovering what actually happens to the *whoosh* of anxiety when left to its own devices.

When allowed to follow its natural course, anxiety does not usually go off the chart and make us feel out of control. The initial surge is intense, and can feel like it is going to continue to escalate forever. In fact, after the initial *whoosh*, anxiety levels out. This is still an incredibly challenging and uncomfortable physical and emotional state, but if we are able to sit with it, what happens next is that the *whoosh* begins to subside on its own.

The more we are able to stay with the feelings of anxiety until the *whoosh* subsides naturally, the more we feel able to do that again the next time.

"Support the person to sit with the *whoosh* of anxiety as it takes hold. This will help them see that they can cope without using their usual behaviours to escape."

This is why addressing avoidance and safety behaviours is so important on the journey toward living better with anxiety. If the person with anxiety can be supported to stay with the *whoosh* without reaching for an escape, they will discover for themselves that, while there are times when it feels like it might, the *whoosh* does not last forever.

HOW TO HELP

- Follow the TURN method, by giving your TIME, and seeking to UNDERSTAND before you proceed to REDIRECTING behaviour.
- It may be that it feels right for you to go straight to REDIRECTING rather than working on REFRAMING thoughts first. It is OK to swap the order of these two, as they are part of the same step.
- Work with the person you are supporting to put together a step-by-step 'exposure' staircase. Each step should be made up of a task or experience that feels a bit more challenging than the last.

- Make sure the tasks on each step are meaningful, and reflect what matters most to the person experiencing anxiety.
- Support them to work through their staircase gradually.
- Look out for the use of avoidance and safety behaviours. If you notice they are adopting safety behaviours to manage the anxiety brought about by the task, support them to consider letting these go.
- Support the person you are helping to sit with the *whoosh* of anxiety as it takes hold. This will help them see that they can cope without using their usual behaviours to escape. We will learn techniques to help with sitting with anxiety in the next chapter.
- If taking on one of the tasks without safety behaviours feels overwhelming for the person you are helping, it might indicate that the level of difficulty is too high for that moment in time. You can revise the staircase at any time to make sure the steps feel even in terms of difficulty and progression.
- Celebrate successes! This process is a massive step toward living well with anxiety. Every achievement is significant, and worthy of celebration.

SUMMARY

- Avoidance and safety behaviours offer relief in the short-term, but ultimately keep anxiety going.
- Addressing avoidance and safety behaviours should be done gradually, and through working together with the person you are supporting.
- Taking a graded approach out of avoidance can be an important step toward living better with anxiety.
- The exposure staircase is a way of gradually building tolerance to the *whoosh* of anxiety. With each step the person takes, they build their confidence, and feel able to take the next step.

CHAPTER 8

PRACTICAL APPROACHES

So, where do we go now? We know that anxiety is an interaction between thoughts, emotions, physical responses and behaviour. We know that anxiety is natural and has a crucial function of keeping us safe. We know that anxiety hurts because it threatens what matters to us, and gets in the way of us living the life we want. And most of all, we know that the best way to support and empower someone living with anxiety is to provide our time, empathy and understanding.

Our three case studies have illustrated a number of things:

In Catriona's case, we have seen that beliefs about personal inadequacy have led to fear and dread around evaluation, to the point that university life has become almost impossible. Striving and seeking perfection might help Catriona escape a sense of failure in the short-term, but ultimately it has kept her caught in a cycle of seeking perfection, and then feeling not good enough and fearing the consequences of that.

For George, we have recognized that fear about his own health and safety, and anxiety around the wellbeing of his family, has locked him into a cycle of avoidance, checking and reassurance-seeking. We know that this is affecting his close relationships, and that he is missing out on enjoying his retirement along the way.

We have seen that Mishka's physical health problems have led her to see herself as vulnerable and unable to cope, and she is managing this by avoiding all the things she used to enjoy. As time has gone on, it has become more and more scary for her to contemplate returning to her old life, and this is taking a toll on her relationships and her wellbeing.

In this chapter, we are going to look at some practical tools and approaches that you can work through with the person you are supporting to help them manage anxiety in a new way. And I hope that by doing so, they can be empowered to live more fully, in a life that is not dominated by trying to control anxiety.

REVISITING THE TURN APPROACH

All of the approaches, ideas and techniques covered in this book come together to be used within the TURN framework for helping someone with anxiety.

Let's remind ourselves of that framework:

- **T**ime
- **U**nderstanding
- **R**eframing and Redirecting
- **N**ew Approach

As well as taking time, listening, reaching a shared understanding, supporting the reframing of perspective and redirection of behaviour, it can be helpful to explore further ways of coping.

The fourth and final step in the TURN method is NEW APPROACH. This means finding techniques and perspectives that take the person you are supporting in a new direction that help them move out of old anxiety patterns, and toward living a free, full and rich life, in the presence of anxiety.

In this chapter, I am going to share with you some of the techniques I see having the strongest effect in empowering my clients to live better with anxiety.

Remember, different things work well for different people at different times. It is important that, when supporting someone with anxiety, you take the stance of offering tools and techniques as suggestions, rather than as a guaranteed 'solution'. The following tasks are offered as ways to help you support someone to build up a suite of coping strategies that make up their New Approach for managing anxiety.

PLANNING FOR CHANGE

One of the most important conversations I have with my clients at the start of therapy is about goals. Before we talk about goals, it is interesting to have a conversation about what is *not* working. Often, it is the frustrations and disappointments that anxiety creates in our lives that points us toward the things that matter most, and that we most want to change.

"Identifying what anxiety costs us, and how that hurts us, is a good way to lead in to a conversation about change."

Let's look at this in relation to Mishka:

Mishka's anxiety has affected just about every area of her life. In conversation with her partner Emma, she reflected on this, and some of the things she identified as particularly painful were:

- *Not being able to go to the gym unaccompanied.*
- *Missing the satisfaction of doing her job.*
- *Reduced self-confidence as a result of not being at work, and not being part of a team.*
- *Feeling disconnected from friends and family.*
- *Not being able to do things spontaneously, like go on a night out or a trip.*

Identifying what anxiety costs us, and how that hurts us, is a good way to lead in to a conversation about change. Once the person you are supporting has talked through the ways in which anxiety gets in the way of them having the life they want, they may be ready to think about how they *do* want things to be.

Like anything in life, setting goals helps us focus on where we want to get to. Identifying a destination – or at least milestones – on any journey is key to making sure we are heading in the right direction.

SETTING REALISTIC GOALS

When I explore with clients who live with anxiety what they want to get out of therapy, I often hear that they want to get rid of anxiety! That is an understandable response.

But think about what would happen if you approached the beginning of a journey by specifying where you do NOT want to end up. It would not provide a great deal of focus. Generally, it is better to identify where you DO want to end up. So when I talk about goals with my clients, I challenge them to think about what they DO want.

If a client says to me their goal is to get rid of anxiety, or to be free of anxiety, my next question is, what would that allow you to have more of? Or what would that let you do that you are not able to do right now?

That can help clarify where we want to end up on our journey, and that serves as a guide for making changes.

Let's take a look at what Mishka wanted:

When exploring goals, it was clear for Mishka that getting back to some of the things she values most in her life would be an important step. With Emma's help, she was able to identify what mattered most to her, and the fundamental values included:

- *Having meaningful connections with people, animals and the wider community.*
- *Being free to make the most of life.*
- *Living a healthy and active life.*

By getting clear on those values, Emma and Mishka could reach a deeper understanding of the suffering that went along with Mishka's anxiety. Anxiety was causing Mishka to become increasingly distanced from the life she wanted to be living; it made sense that that would hurt.

Getting clear on values in this way is an excellent foundation for thinking about specific goals. When goals are rooted in an understanding of WHY something hurts us, we are more able to commit to making changes. In other words, establishing the outcome we want puts our eyes on the prize. This galvanizes change, and directs the focus of the work that needs to be done to get there.

Now, let's look at Mishka's goals:

Having got clear on what mattered to her the most, and thought about how anxiety was holding her back, Mishka came up with the following goals for living better with anxiety:

- *Gradually return to work, building up to full-time over a three-month period.*
- *Be able to accept invitations to spend time with family at Christmas.*

- *Attend a weekly gym class regularly, and be able to attend unaccompanied.*
- *Meet up with close friends for dinner at a favourite restaurant for Emma's birthday.*
- *Get out into the hills with Emma and the dogs at least once a month.*
- *Be able to do things spontaneously without anxiety getting in the way.*

You will notice that these goals have some things in common. They all relate to clear tasks or activities, and include a commitment to when they will happen, or how often they will happen where that is possible. They are also aligned with the things that truly matter to Mishka.

When setting goals, it is important to set them in time and to keep them fairly concrete. Notice the difference between these two goals:

1. See friends more.
2. Meet up with close friends for dinner at a favourite restaurant for Emma's birthday.

The second goal is more specific than the first. It details activity, people, place and a point in time.

We are all more likely to stick with a goal if it relates to specific events and tasks. Therefore, helping the person you are supporting to come up with goals at this level of detail sets them up to succeed. Of course, goals can be changed or amended at any time, and you can add new goals whenever you want. The important thing is that they reflect what matters most to the person living with anxiety.

"Encourage reflection on the areas of their life that are affected by anxiety."

Goals give us a useful guide and a reminder of the outcome we are supporting the other person to achieve. When we think of our New Approach, it is useful to bear in mind what goals the person has identified. That way, you can always check in with whether they feel they are moving toward or away from where they want to end up.

Goals provide a brilliant basis for focusing change. When the person is clear on goals, you can both use that clarity to inform the New Approach you build together.

HOW TO HELP

- Encourage the person you are supporting to reflect on the areas of their life that are affected by anxiety.
- Focus on what they would like more of in their life. Beware setting goals around what they want to avoid. Remember, your journey needs a clear destination!

- Keep goals specific, linked to behaviour and rooted in time as much as you can.
- Make sure the goals you set together reflect what matters most to the person you are helping.
- Use goals as a guide or map for progress.
- Remember, goals can be altered or changed at any time. The important thing is that they reflect what truly matters to the person you are supporting.

COPING WITH WORRY

Worry and anxiety often go hand-in-hand. When I am working with clients to help them live better with anxiety, we often end up having some interesting conversations about worry.

Many of us carry a belief that worrying is a useful way to keep ourselves safe. I often hear people say things like, 'If I didn't worry, I wouldn't be prepared for when things go wrong' or 'If I didn't worry, I might drop the ball and forget about some important things I need to take care of.'

It is important to recognize that some worry can be useful in making us take action to address important things. For example, worrying about an upcoming interview can make us prepare to a higher standard. Worrying about paperwork we have not yet completed can make us get it done on time. Part of recognizing the seriousness of some situations in life can involve thinking through options, feeling a degree of anxiety about the possibility of a bad outcome, and looking ahead to make contingency plans for worst-case scenarios.

But there is a difference between recognizing the seriousness of a situation, or taking reasonable steps to keep ourselves safe, and becoming consumed with thoughts about worst-case scenarios that tip us into panic, and cause anxiety storms to spiral and escalate. This is what can happen when planning or consideration turns into a repetitive and unproductive mental behaviour, focused on potential future outcomes, which is ultimately what worry is.

"Worry check: ask the person you are supporting to consider if there is value in spending time going over and over the same worries."

For many people living with anxiety, worry is an insidious presence that spreads into mental and emotional space like gas filling a room.

Worry is usually triggered by uncertainty. When we are faced with an ambiguous or uncertain situation, rather than sit with the uncertainty, we are likely to go over possible outcomes to try to manufacture a sense of certainty for ourselves. The problem with this is that our mind often jumps to worst-case scenarios, and then we get pulled into an extended anxiety storm, reacting to what our mind has given us as if it were true.

We've seen this with George:

Worry has become an increasingly prominent part of George's experience of anxiety. When he faces any ambiguity or uncertainty, his mind generates worst-case scenarios, and he goes over these in detail, imagining all the terrible things that could happen. Quickly, this becomes a full-blown anxiety storm.

When the mind is focused on an imagined future, not only do we have to deal with the emotional effects of the things we imagine could happen, we also miss out on being fully present and attentive in the here and now.

It is not uncommon for me to hear people who experience anxiety tell me that they also have a bad memory. I ask them to consider this: if your mind is off in the future, how can it attend to information in the present? And if you are not attending to information in the present, how can you expect your mind to take in new information and store it for you?

Broadly speaking, worry can be divided into two categories.

1. The first kind of worry is helpful or productive worry. That is the kind of worry that drives us to do things to keep

ourselves safe, and to put sensible precautions in place in the face of a threat. It is the kind of worry that motivates us to address problems, and engage with important tasks.

2. Unhelpful or unproductive worry is the type that can escalate and involves us into going over and over worst-case scenarios in our minds, without leading to positive action. This type of worry tends to be repetitive, and can cause us to feel trapped. This can be accompanied by feelings of anxiety, panic, dread and helplessness.

HOW TO HELP

- Worry check – ask the person you are supporting to consider if there is value in spending time going over and over the same worries.
- Be open to their beliefs about worry. They may believe that worry protects them or helps keep them safe. Be careful to validate this perspective, before you introduce any form of challenge.
- Support the person to identify what they can control, and take the steps necessary to address that part of the situation.
- Ask if their worry is something you can reasonably address or resolve in the short-term?
- If the answer to that is yes, help them work out what steps they may need to take to do that.

- If the answer is no, gently remind them that time spent worrying is unlikely to resolve the issue.
- Encourage them to take a few minutes to note their worries, and then to put that note away. They can return to look at the note at a later time if they wish.
- Be aware that it may not be helpful to spend a lot of time going over and over the person's worries with them in conversation. If you notice conversations becoming repetitive, or the person's anxiety escalates in the conversation, it may be time to redirect the focus to what action can be taken.
- Worry can be contagious. If you notice your own mood or anxiety level being negatively impacted by engaging in worry-focused conversation, take a step back.

BREATHING

The fight-or-flight response – and the *whoosh* of physical experiences that go with it – is at the heart of the experience of anxiety. Anxiety happens in the body, and one of the most powerful tools we have to regulate anxiety also involves the body. That tool is breathing.

I am sometimes wary of introducing breathing exercises in therapy, because breathing as an exercise has perhaps become a cliché or a way of brushing off the depth of suffering lived through by people who experience anxiety. It is not enough to direct someone who is at the height of an anxiety storm to 'just breathe'.

Having said that, introduced in the context of the TURN method, breathing has the potential to be one of the most powerful tools you can support the person you are helping to put into practice.

"Breathing is the key to restoring balance in the body during an anxiety storm and a good tool to use when it is starting to brew."

First, let's have a quick recap of why breathing is so important. Earlier in the book, we looked in detail at how the fight-or-flight response is responsible for the collection of physical experiences that often go with anxiety (see page 54). When the internal fire signal is activated and the *whoosh* of anxiety takes over, lots of things happen in our bodies, with the function of preparing us to fight a predator or run away from a predator.

Breathing is the key to restoring balance in the body during an anxiety storm and a good tool to use when it is starting to brew, because it can slow the escalation of a storm and keep the body from being taken over with the physical feelings of anxiety.

Here is a simple breathing exercise that can help to get the body back onto an even keel. Try out these exercises first yourself, and then consider sharing them with the person you are supporting.

EXERCISE
Simple Breathing

Start by breathing in through the nose for a count of five.

Then hold the breath for a count of five.

And release for a count of five, gently through the mouth as if you are blowing out a candle.

Repeat five times.

When supporting someone to use breathing techniques, it can be useful to help them look at *how* they breathe. When we feel anxious or tense, we tend to take shallow breaths – that is breathing into the top of chest, and no further. A sign of shallow breathing is that the top part of the torso rises and falls noticeably, as if all the air is staying in the top part of the torso.

For deep breathing to have an effect, it is important that the breath makes it all the way down to the lower part of the torso.

EXERCISE
Balloon Breathing

Start by imagining that there is an empty balloon in your stomach, with the opening at the very top of your stomach, at the bottom of the chest, and the balloon hanging down from there. Decide on a colour for your balloon.

Before you start the breathing part of the exercise, take a moment to remind yourself of the image of a balloon being inflated. Notice not only that the balloon gets bigger, but also that the colour appears to fade as the latex stretches. And when the balloon deflates, it returns to its original size and colour.

Now, picturing the empty balloon hanging, breathe in for a count of five. As you breathe in, imagine the air is filling up the balloon.

As the air travels in, picture the balloon inflating gradually. Notice the size and colour of the balloon change.

Notice your stomach rise with every count. After five counts, hold the filled-up balloon in your mind for a count of five.

Then release by blowing gently through the mouth, picturing the balloon reducing in size and intensifying in colour, until it has returned to its original state.

Repeat five times.

One way to check if this is happening is to put a hand on your stomach when you practise breathing exercises and notice if there is a rise and fall with the breath.

The exercise on page 163 can help get the breath into the lower part of the body. This is my own go-to exercise, and the one I most enjoy sharing with my clients.

The balloon image has a dual purpose. Firstly, imagining the balloon being positioned in the lower part of the abdomen helps direct the breath there, which means the exercise will have a greater balancing effect. In addition, having to picture the changing state of the balloon, and keep up with counting, occupies the mind during the exercise. This offers a temporary change of focus, away from anxiety-based thoughts long enough for the body to get back to a more balanced state.

HOW TO HELP

- Invite your loved one to join you in trying out the breathing exercises in this chapter.
- Encourage them to practise breathing exercises when their anxiety is at a manageable level. This will help them put the exercises into practice during more difficult times.

- When you notice the person you are helping is in the grip of an anxiety storm, try using a breathing exercise as a NEW APPROACH, as part of the TURN method.

GETTING INTO THE PRESENT MOMENT

In the grip of an anxiety storm, the mind is rarely focusing on the present. When we face uncertainty or threat, the mind automatically comes up with imagined future scenarios and outcomes, and we engage with those as if they are real and true.

Often, this means that part of anxiety involves our minds being focused on an imagined future.

In George's case, imagining what might go wrong on a trip; in Catriona's case, imagining failing university.

Our inner threat system does not know the difference between an immediate threat in front of us in real life and the threatening situations our minds think up when we worry and catastrophize.

Our anxious minds tend to live in the future, imagining the worst. This is why using techniques to consciously bring our focus back to the present can be a useful way to manage anxiety. If we can catch our minds before negative thoughts snowball completely, we can use that as an exit strategy in an anxiety storm, or even use it to stop a full storm gathering in the first place.

'Grounding' means using the senses to connect with what is around us, to bring our attention to the present moment. In other words, turning our focus from our busy minds, and toward what we can sense in our environment, at this very moment in time.

Take a moment to notice your own environment, right now, as you sit and read this book. Notice that, when you do that, your attention moves into the present.

The following grounding exercise is a simple way to help someone bring their focus away from racing thoughts concerned with an imagined future, and into the present. You can use this on its own, or as part of a NEW APPROACH within the TURN framework.

EXERCISE
Grounding

Take a moment to stop and take a few deep breaths.
Bring your attention into your immediate physical environment.

Notice one thing you can see.

Notice one thing you can touch.
Notice one thing you can hear.
Repeat this, going through the senses one by one.
Notice that what you are seeing, touching and hearing is real right now.

Bringing our attention into the present moment in this way can interrupt an anxiety storm by moving the focus away from the imagined worst-case scenarios and into the present moment.

HOW TO HELP

- Encourage the person you are supporting to practise a grounding exercise when their anxiety is at a manageable level. This will help them put the practice into use during more difficult times.
- When you notice the person you are supporting is in the grip of an anxiety storm, try using a grounding exercise as a NEW APPROACH, when using the TURN method.
- Remember to encourage them to use breathing and grounding the help them manage rises in anxiety that go with working through their anxiety staircase, or other challenges.

SUMMARY

- Supporting the person to identify their goals is a good way of clarifying the way forward. Knowing where you want to end up usually makes it easier to get there!
- Separating what is controllable from what is not controllable is an important step for managing worry.
- Breathing and grounding techniques are a useful tool for bringing focus into the present moment, and stepping out of anxious thoughts.
- You can help the person you are supporting to connect with breathing and grounding exercises at any point. Mastering these tools can often be a very empowering step on the journey to living well with anxiety.

CHAPTER 9

BRINGING IT ALL TOGETHER

I hope that by now you have a sense of how you might approach helping someone with anxiety. Now that we have walked together through the stages of the TURN method, we are going to take a look at how we can put it all into practice in order to help the person you are supporting live better with anxiety.

Let's look at how Helen used the TURN method to help George:

George and Helen have been invited to the 60th birthday party of one of George's oldest friends. From the moment the invitation arrived, George felt a sense of panic and dread. At the same time, a big part of him very much wanted to go to the party.

By using the TURN method, Helen helped George see that his anxiety was a natural response because the trip would involve some uncertainties. She was also able to help him see that maintaining connections with old friends was important, because having meaningful friendships is something that matters a great deal to George. Being at the party had the potential to bring a lot of enjoyment and connections. Through those realizations, Helen and George agreed a goal of attending the party.

On the days leading up to the party, George found his mind was consumed with worry about the trip. His mind raced with thoughts of what would happen if something went wrong on the journey. What if they got a flat tyre? What if the weather caused a problem? Helen noticed that George seemed more and more preoccupied as the event drew near. She also noticed that George was irritable and stressed, and that he seemed tense.

George started complaining that he was worried he was coming down with something because he was feeling warm and lightheaded. The more George noticed these physical symptoms, the more tense he became. Previously, Helen would have managed the situation by cancelling the trip and making an excuse to their friends about why there were unable to be there.

Here is how Helen applied the TURN method to try out a new way of helping:

- *Time – first, Helen gently mentioned to George that she noticed he seemed preoccupied and stressed. She took time to listen to his fears about the trip without criticism or judgement.*

- **U**nderstanding – *Together, Helen and George were able to recognize that going into an unknown situation was anxiety-provoking for George. They identified that George was worrying about the journey, and that this was causing activation of his fight-or-flight response.*
- **R**eframing and Redirecting – *Helen was able to help George recognize that his physical experiences may be related to a fight-or-flight response, rather than there being anything wrong with him physically. Together, she and George identified that his mind was catastrophizing about the trip. Helen was able to challenge the urge to cancel the trip. She recognized that this would be avoidance and saw that, while that might bring some relief to George in the short-term, it would feed into his anxiety in the longer-term.*
- **N**ew Approach – *Helen supported George to distinguish productive worry from unproductive worry. This led to Helen and George identifying clear steps they could reasonably take to make their journey safe. They agreed that checking the tyre pressure on the car before they set off, making sure they had enough fuel for the journey and identifying their route in advance would be reasonable precautions to take prior to setting off.*

As they prepared to depart, Helen noticed that George seemed tense and anxious. Again, she used the TURN method to support George:

- **Ti**me – First, she paused to give George an opportunity to share how he was feeling, and to listen to him without judgement. In that conversation Helen shared that she, too, felt a bit nervous about the trip, because it had been a long time since they had travelled for a social occasion.
- **U**nderstanding – Again, Helen helped George recognize that anxiety about the trip was natural, and that his body was feeling the effects of the fight-or-flight response.
- **R**eframing and Redirecting – Helen and George were able to remind themselves that going on the trip was important to them, for a number of reasons. They also reminded themselves that cancelling the trip would feed into George's anxiety in the longer-term.
- **N**ew Approach – Helen supported George to practise some breathing and grounding techniques to help bring him out of a brewing anxiety storm. With Helen's support, George was also able to use these techniques to keep anxiety storms at bay during the journey and the party.

As a result, George achieved his goal of attending the party. Anxiety was with him throughout, but he was able to manage it and noticed a growth in confidence having managed to go through with it.

The enjoyment of catching up with old friends and being part of the celebration made putting up with the discomfort of anxiety worth it. On their journey home, George and Helen reflected on how glad they were that they had gone ahead with the trip.

"I know the feeling of seeing how much someone is struggling, knowing that there are things that could potentially help, but the person not yet being ready to take the necessary steps."

DEALING WITH RESISTANCE

You may be thinking the TURN method is all very well if someone close to you is asking for help, and willingly engaging with your efforts. But what do you do if the person you want to support is not yet ready to take steps toward making a change, and not yet ready to look for support or accept help? What do you do if your efforts to help are met with resistance or ambivalence? Sometimes, if we push someone to get help before they are ready, it can make them even more closed to the idea of accepting support.

As the supporter of someone living with anxiety, this is an extremely difficult position in which to find yourself. You want to help, you are taking steps to learn how you can help, and yet the person you want to support is not responding to your efforts. Or worse, your efforts seem to put distance between you and the person you want to help, as they shut down or withdraw when you try to address what is going on.

It might be that the person experiencing anxiety is able to recognize their difficulties, but does not yet feel ready or able to take active steps toward making a change.

This situation can make you feel powerless. As a therapist, and personally, I know the feeling of seeing how much someone is struggling, knowing that there are things that could potentially help, but the person not yet being ready to take the necessary steps.

"Don't underestimate the value of being present. This, above all else, is the most powerful asset you have for helping someone with anxiety."

WE CAN'T 'MAKE IT BETTER'

Let's go back to thinking about connection. You picked up this book because you want to learn to respond to the person with anxiety in a helpful way. Don't underestimate the value of being present with the other person, and letting them know that you want to support them. This, above all else, is the most powerful asset you have for helping the person close to you. Whether you are connecting online or by phone from a distance, or you are together in person, your presence matters above all else.

Let's look at how this might apply for Mishka and Emma:

There are times when Mishka becomes so consumed with feelings of fear and anxiety that Emma, as her main supporter, feels helpless and lost. When Mishka is caught in an anxiety storm, or feeling particularly low on motivation and becoming withdrawn, Emma's urge is to try to bring some positivity to the situation.

In the past, one way Emma has approached this is by offering up more and more strategies, alternative perspectives and suggested activities to Mishka to try to get her out of her distressed state. However, Emma has learned that doing this creates distance rather than connection in Mishka's deepest suffering. In this kind of situation, Mishka's apparent lack of willingness to try is frustrating for Emma.

"When we are in a helping role, it is easy to get stuck on the idea that we need to be *doing* something that leads to the person we are supporting to *feel better*."

Before we look at how the TURN method can be used in this kind of situation, let's remember our objective throughout this book is to *help* someone with anxiety.

When we are in a helping role, it is easy to get stuck on the idea that we need to be *doing* something that leads to the person we are supporting to *feel better*. This still happens to me now, nearly 15 years since I started working as a therapist. I still get times where I question my own effectiveness if I am not *making it better* for the person I am working with. Sometimes we all need a reminder that escaping difficult feelings is not the only valid way of supporting someone who is suffering.

With that in mind, let's think about how the TURN method can be applied when distress is high, when motivation is low, or when the person you are supporting says, 'I don't want to.'

Here's how Emma applied the TURN method:

Mishka had planned to meet a good friend for a coffee, but the anxiety leading up to it had become so intense that she decided to cancel. As a result, Mishka felt temporary relief from anxiety, but soon that was replaced with thoughts about potentially having offended her friend, and a return to anxiety, along with sadness and despair.

In order to try to help, Emma turned to her usual strategy of offering alternative perspectives, and suggesting things to do. This made Mishka feel more anxious and upset, because she was already anxious and feeling down. Recognizing that this 'doing' approach was not going to be helpful in that moment, Emma, used the TURN method to enhance connection and help Mishka sit with her difficult feelings.

- **T**ime – Emma made time to be present with Mishka, and to fully hear the extent of her distress with empathy. She resisted any urge to impose positivity or dismiss Mishka's feelings. She offered space and validation. By taking her time, Emma, was able to create an opportunity for calm and connection between herself and Mishka.
- **U**nderstanding – Emma was able to recognize that Mishka was in the grip of an anxiety storm and stuck on negative, anxiety-based thoughts. She realized Mishka was not ready to challenge thoughts or experiment with new behaviours at that time.
- **R**eframing and Redirecting – Emma could see that Mishka may not at that moment be ready to look at

evidence or try exposure. Instead, she offered Mishka the simple reminder that they could work together to sit with her difficult feelings.

- ***N**ew Approach – Together, Emma and Mishka completed some simple breathing exercises. In doing so, they sat with Mishka's distress, in unity, and rode through the anxiety storm, without fighting it.*

By showing the other person that we are able to tolerate their pain without trying to escape it, we can strengthen our connection with them and build trust. This means that when the person's distress is a little less intense, they may be in a better place to think about goals, and about change.

HOW TO HELP

- Remember the value of being present with the person you are supporting, in person or at a distance, and letting them know that you want to help them.
- Beware getting caught up with the idea that helping someone *escape* anxiety is the only way to help them with anxiety.
- Use the TURN method to be present with the person in their distress, and in their stuck-ness.
- Make use of coping strategies such as breathing and

grounding exercises to support the person through their distress.

- Remember, you can return to looking at goals, evidence, exposure and other tasks when the person you are helping is ready. If you push it when they are not ready, you will risk putting distance between you.

SUMMARY

- Different applications of the TURN method will work in different situations.
- As the person who is close to someone with anxiety, you will know best about what approach to take and when.
- Sometimes, the person you are supporting may not be ready to actively make a change to their thinking or behaviour. In this situation, the most empowering thing you can do is support them to sit through the surge of anxiety.
- Remember, noticing thought patterns is a powerful reframe in its own right.
- Similarly, sitting with anxiety (instead of seeking to escape it) can be a powerful redirecting of behaviour.

CHAPTER 10

WHEN TO SEEK
PROFESSIONAL HELP

My hope is that by putting the TURN method into practice, you will be able to build a connection with the person you are supporting that leads to some positive shifts for them, and perhaps some improvements in your own quality of life.

Depending on the circumstances of the person with anxiety, it may be that despite your good intentions and compassionate work, a more formal intervention is needed to help them move forward. If you find that their difficulties with anxiety are steadily worsening, and that they are increasingly distressed, it may be time to consider how you might guide the person you are supporting to seek additional help.

There are lots of options to consider, and ultimately only the person themselves can decide what help they want to seek. However, having some information about options can help with making an informed choice.

By picking up this book, you have already taken an important step to empower yourself to help the person close to you who is struggling. However, it may be that they would benefit from a self-help guide that focuses on helping them help themselves, by directly teaching coping skills and other ways of dealing with anxiety.

Accessing direct self-help in this way is often a good first step for someone who is ready to start making a change. Some recommended self-help reading is listed at the end of this book (see page 216). This may be a good starting point if you would like to direct the person you are supporting to some useful resources.

If anxiety is affecting your loved one's life to the point that they are not able to do the things they would usually do (such as maintain their relationships, socialize, and go to work), then it may be time to consider whether a formal therapeutic intervention might be a good option.

Often, the first port of call for professional help is the person's doctor, who is likely to ask if they have tried anything to help already, such as self-help. The doctor may discuss medication options and explore the possibility of a referral to 'talking therapy'.

Cognitive Behavioural Therapy (CBT) is one type of talking therapy that would commonly be offered to someone who is struggling with anxiety. Most of the approaches covered in this book are rooted in CBT. There is evidence indicating that CBT is an effective therapy for anxiety,[ix] and it is usually delivered within a time-limited framework, which is why it tends to be a commonly available therapy through healthcare services. That is not to say that there are not other therapies that can be very effective and may be available, depending on local provision.

Therapy might be offered in a number of different formats. The following list outlines some of the most common modalities in which therapy may be available. However, it is likely this will vary across different areas. The best way to find out about what services are offered by the health services in your area is via the website for your healthcare provider, or through your doctor's surgery.

Some of the ways in which healthcare services might be able to provide help with anxiety are:

Self-help materials: This might include information leaflets or self-help resources for the person to work through to learn about managing anxiety. This can be a good way of getting some information about anxiety from a reliable source.

Computerized therapy programmes: Sometimes, help is offered in the form of access to a computerized therapy programme, which may involve a mixture of reading, virtual interaction and practical skills. This can be a good way of benefitting from therapeutic techniques and approaches in a virtual space, and a particularly good starting point for those who may struggle to get out or to attend appointments in person.

Education classes: Some healthcare settings may offer classroom-type sessions, where people can learn coping strategies. In this setting, those attending are not expected to participate as such, but to come along and learn from the therapist taking the class, like you would attending a public talk or lecture. Classes are a good way of learning ways to cope with anxiety, and attending as part of a group (even if you don't speak to anyone!) can be a powerful way to challenge stigma or shame around anxiety and seeking help.

Group therapy: Therapy is sometimes offered in a smaller, interactive group setting, which involves attending for a set number of sessions with the same group of people, and sharing some of your difficulties. In this type of setting, a facilitator or therapist will lead the sessions, and the group might work through a protocol for dealing with anxiety. Sharing experiences of anxiety with others in a therapeutic space can be a great opportunity to normalize difficult experiences. This kind of group can also open up opportunities for mutual support and learning.

Individual psychological therapy: In some cases, individual therapy may be offered. Usually, this will be a time-limited piece of work, focusing specifically on anxiety. However, in cases where the person's anxiety might be linked to earlier life adversity or trauma, longer-term individual psychological therapy might be offered.

Private therapy: Some people may want to consider seeking therapeutic help privately. There are a number of advantages to this, such as being able to choose the type of therapy, the therapist and the duration of input. It also means you will be able to access help almost right away, which can be an important factor especially if waiting times elsewhere are a concern. Online therapy options such as remote therapy via video call can overcome obstacles to do with location.

However, one major consideration around accessing private therapy is cost. If you have private health insurance, it is worth checking whether it covers therapy. Some practitioners may also offer a reduced fee for those on lower incomes. But unfortunately, cost can be a significant barrier for some people wishing to access therapy privately.

In addition to one-to-one private therapy, some independent practitioners have self-help packages and online courses available to purchase. Again, the advantage is being able to choose depending on the provider and what is offered within their package or course.

A NOTE OF CAUTION

There is an abundance of practitioners who offer help with anxiety and other mental health issues. While some advertising sites usually require practitioners to provide proof of their qualifications and professional accreditation, it is possible for anyone to market themselves as a 'therapist' or 'coach', and to write a course or self-help guide and sell it.

> "Take time with the person you are supporting to consider the options for help available. Different things work for different people at different times. Support them to think about what might work best for them."

When looking into options for private therapy – be that through individual therapy or self-help approaches – I would strongly recommend that you encourage the person you are supporting to check out the credentials of whoever they are considering. To select an appropriate professional who is trustworthy, it is advisable to check their qualifications and professional accreditation.

There are different accrediting bodies for different professionals working in the field of therapy. When a professional is a member of an accrediting body, they are bound to the professional standards of that body, related to important things like ethical practice, confidentiality and professionalism. A suitably qualified and accredited practitioner will not mind being asked about their credentials and will be happy to provide supporting evidence.

HOW TO HELP

- If it seems the difficulties of the person you are supporting have gone beyond what you and they can manage together, encourage them to consider speaking to their doctor.
- Take time with them to consider the options for help available. Different things work for different people at different times. Support them to think about what might work best for them.
- If the person you are supporting is considering accessing private help, encourage them to look for evidence of a professional qualification and, ideally, membership of an accrediting body or some other form of professional validation.
- When the person you are supporting begins therapy, take an interest and offer to support them with any tasks they are asked to complete between sessions.
- Remember you can remain a sounding board and valuable support while they go through therapy.

DEEP DESPAIR AND HOPELESSNESS

When we open up a different kind of conversation, we don't know where it might lead. When we make ourselves available by giving time and understanding, we can create the conditions for someone to go deeper with what they share with us.

Whether we expect it or not, sometimes connecting at a deeper level of conversation can uncover feelings of despair and hopelessness, which the person has not previously shared.

If the person you want to help tells you that they feel hopeless, trapped, that they feel they are too much of a burden to those around them or that life is not worth living, it is more important than ever that you listen without judgement.

> "It is important to resist any urge to focus on positivity or try to 'lighten up' the conversation. If you can, go to where it is darkest, and sit with the person in their pain."

Seeing someone you care about in such a dark place is not an easy thing to cope with. The most helpful thing you can do is stay calm and stay open to what they are telling you. More than ever, it is important to resist any urge to focus on positivity or try to 'lighten up' the conversation. If you can, go to where it is darkest, and sit with the person in their pain.

Believe me when I say I know this takes courage.

There are some questions it is important to ask the person you are supporting if you think they might be feeling suicidal. The first is, 'Are you feeling suicidal?'

Sometimes it can feel risky to ask that question because we worry that we might put the idea in the person's head and make them more likely to think about suicide. But evidence tells us that asking about suicide does not make the person more likely to think about suicide or act on suicidal thoughts.ˣ Again, I know it takes courage to ask this question, but it could save the person's life.

If the person you are supporting tells you that they are suicidal, try not to panic. The fact that they have felt able to be honest about that with you is a good thing, and you are now in a position to help them.

If you can, ask them how far down that line of thought they have gone. This information could be important for helping to keep them safe. If they disclose to you that they have actioned a plan, for example by gathering certain things or making specific arrangements, let them share that information with you.

If the person tells you that they are suicidal and that they have an immediate plan to hurt themselves, here are the things you can do to help keep them safe:

- Stay calm, stay in the conversation and remember it is OK to talk about suicide.
- Gently, and without judgement, gather as much information as you can about any plans they have to hurt themselves or end their life.

- Reassure them that you want to help them get through this.
- Talk to them about getting help. Together, make a plan for how they will access that help, offering your support to do so if they want that.
- Keep the conversation open.

If someone is in crisis, and telling you they are planning to take action to end their life right away, here are some things you can do to help keep them safe:

- Stay with them.
- If you are not speaking in person, encourage them to confide in someone who may be able to support them in person, alongside your own support.
- Keep talking about how they are feeling, without judgement.
- Remove any items that they may be planning to use to harm themselves.
- If they are in immediate danger, call emergency services.

Nobody expects you to manage this on your own. A big part of your role at this stage will become letting the person know that you are there for them, and working together to take steps to keep them safe by linking in with professional support services.

SUPPORTING SOMEONE WHO IS SUICIDAL

Learning that someone close to us is feeling suicidal can leave us feeling deeply shocked, frightened, distressed and overwhelmed. For that reason, it is crucial to take steps to look after yourself if you find yourself in that position.

First and foremost, remember that while there are some things you can do to help the person close to you, it is not solely your responsibility to know how they are feeling, or to keep them safe. Of course you want to do everything you can, but equally, be prepared to accept help and support from services, and from other supporters if that is possible.

Self-care matters more than ever in this situation. That means considering your own needs, and making use of the resources you have around you. Speaking to someone in confidence is one of the most powerful ways to process things and get support. Trusted friends or family members might provide that for you, but if not there are organizations ready to listen. The names of some organizations are listed at the end of the book.

SUMMARY

- It may be that, despite your help, the person that you are suporting requires professional help with anxiety or related difficulties.

- There is a range of options that you can consider, with different levels of accessibility and at different levels of intensity.
- It is recommended to check the credentials of any professional who is offering mental health care, interventions or treatment packages.
- If you are concerned the person you are helping may be suicidal, listen without judgement. If necessary, take steps to help keep them safe.
- It is important to access professional help if someone is suicidal.
- You are in an emotionally demanding position. Be kind to yourself, and access support.

CHAPTER 11

YOUR ROLE IN RECOVERY

Perhaps one of the most painful realizations on the journey of helping someone close to us comes when we encounter the limits to what we can influence and what we can control. I think this can be particularly difficult when we are trying to help a grown-up child, because we have spent their entire lives trying to protect them and do our best for them.

It makes sense that the more stuck someone seems, the more you want to *do* something to make things better for them. And I recognize that, by encouraging you to stay with them in their distress, rather than focus on fixing, I am suggesting something that might be counterintuitive, and extremely difficult.

Perhaps one of the hardest things about training to be a therapist or psychologist is learning how to sit with someone's suffering. I have heard it called *getting comfortable with being uncomfortable.*

"Sitting with discomfort may be one of the most helpful things you can do to help the person close to you. But I want to acknowledge how difficult that is."

This book is not intended to train you as a therapist, and it would not be right to expect you to feel OK with the pain and suffering of the person you are helping, when that is something that many (maybe most) therapists can find difficult.

And, yet, sitting with discomfort may be one of the most helpful things you can do to help the person you are supporting. I want to acknowledge how difficult that is, and to say that it is OK to struggle with that. Bearing witness to someone's pain, and sitting with them in their struggle, can have a deep personal effect. For that reason, I want to remind you that this journey is a challenging one, and one that is not without cost to you, as the helper.

Ultimately, there is a balance to be struck between constructive determination, and recognizing the limit to what you can do to help.

This was certainly the experience of Catriona's mother, Angela:

Along with her husband Robert, Angela has tried to do everything she can to help their daughter, Catriona. It was heartbreaking for Robert and Angela to learn the full extent of Catriona's struggles. As parents, they had done everything they could to give Catriona, and her two sisters, the best possible start in life. Catriona's difficulties caused Robert and Angela to question whether they may somehow be responsible for what was going on. At times, their frustration at the situation caused them to unwittingly put pressure on Catriona, and this had caused her to grow distant from them.

Angela and Robert considered every possible avenue they could explore in order to help Catriona. They wondered if one of them should move closer to her temporarily, or whether they ought to look into getting her extra tuition to support her studies and help her feel more confident academically. They looked into what therapy might be available. Over time, Angela found herself becoming more and more consumed with trying to find the key that would unlock Catriona's recovery.

Catriona's sisters were concerned about her, and wanted to support her in any way they could. However, over time, they also became increasingly concerned about their parents, as they could see them – especially their mother – becoming more and more stressed and affected by what was going on. They noticed their mum was not participating in her own social life in the way she used to, and began to feel that every conversation and decision revolved around Catriona's anxiety.

FOCUSING ON WHAT YOU CAN CONTROL

One way to work toward this balance is to consider what you can and what you cannot control.

There will no doubt be controllables and uncontrollables specific to your own situation. But to start you off, here are some things you can probably control, and some things which you may not be able to control:

What you can control:

- How you spend your time. It is up to you how you balance time for you, time with the person you are supporting, time for other people and other things.
- You can control the attitude you bring to this relationship, and to your loved one's experience of anxiety. For example, by opening this book, by reading this far into it, and by implementing the principles of the TURN method, you are showing an attitude of willingness to help.
- The extent to which you seek to learn about anxiety is under your control. Again, reading this book is part of that.

- While it may sometimes be challenging, you are in control of your own boundaries. In other words, it is up to you to what extent you make yourself practically and emotionally available to others.

What you may not be able to control:

- The extent to which the person close to you is ready to engage with help.
- The extent to which they are willing to make changes.
- Situational factors influencing the emotional life of the person you want to help, such as their other relationships, the pressure they face at work or in their studies, the choices they make, and when and how they may be impacted by bad news.

DEFINING YOUR HELPING ROLE

Throughout our journey together, I have emphasized giving time, space, validation and empathy. And, undoubtedly, this can be a valuable approach to empowering the other person through connection and shared understanding.

However, it is important to be aware of the potential for your helping role to cross a line into a dynamic that may not be so helpful, and may even be detrimental to you.

"Consider how you can fulfil a helping role while continuing to nurture and protect your existing relationship."

When we set out to help someone, we usually do so because the wellbeing of that person is important to us. But sometimes, our helping role can become a little blurred, especially when the person we are trying to help is someone close to us. In this situation, it is impossible to separate your role as a helper from your broader relationship with the person. It is also impossible to separate that from the wider context of family, friendships or community within which your relationship exists.

For these reasons, it is important to consider how you can fulfil a helping role while continuing to nurture and protect your existing relationship.

Communication is an essential part of maintaining a healthy dynamic. You know that you want to help the person close to you, but in order to give both of you the best possible chance, it is essential that your wish to help is made clear to them right from the beginning and that they give you their consent to take on a helping role. That way, your wish to actively help them with their anxiety is known clearly and explicitly in the relationship between you. That allows them to know and understand your intentions, and it opens up a dialogue about how your helping role will work in the context of your broader relationship.

It is important that you have consent from the person you want to support to take on a helping role. If you step into this role uninvited and impose a helping approach where that is not wanted or welcomed, you could risk putting distance between yourself and the other person, or adding to their stress.

This is an important process because it sets up your helping journey as an open and shared endeavour from the start. The more you and the person you want to support approach this journey as a team, with open communication, the easier it will be to apply the methods and techniques you pick up in the book.

HOW TO HELP

- From the beginning, let the other person know that you would like to help.
- Share with them that you would like to learn more about anxiety, and that you want to be an ally to them in their journey toward learning to live better with anxiety.
- Seek explicit permission from them to take on an informal helping role.
- Approach the work you will do together as a team.
- Talk to them about their expectations of working together in this way and, if possible, share your

expectations. See if you can work toward a common ground of how you want to approach it.

- Resist any urge to be the expert or the one who knows best. Set up your role as a willing helper, emphasizing that you are not offering a substitute for professional therapeutic input.
- Keep communication open and honest. This includes being open to difficult feedback from the person you are supporting. Mutual compassion is key to preserving your relationship.

As you now know, there are parts of the helping role that may involve you gently challenging the person you want to help, such as when you choose not to enable avoidance or safety behaviours. If you have the person's informed consent, you will be in a much stronger position to carry out these parts of the helping process, and this will help protect your relationship with them.

WHEN HELPING BECOMES UNHELPFUL

When we enter a helping role, we can find ourselves taking responsibility for the other person 'getting better'. We can find ourselves increasingly preoccupied with the person's difficulties, and what we can do to help. We can begin to feel that it is our job, alone, to find the key that unlocks the solution that will transform the other person's situation.

If we view things from this perspective, we can find that our purpose and identity become increasingly entwined with our ability to help the other person. With that, there may be a risk that our self-worth, and our view of ourselves as a parent, partner, or friend starts to depend on the extent to which we are able to help.

Within this dynamic, we may find ourselves seeking to 'rescue' the other person, which may involve us seeking to remove the burden of any responsibility from them, under the guise of giving them less to feel anxious about.

If this dynamic continues over time, we are increasingly at risk of becoming locked into an unhelpful pattern, where we are defined by the other person's need for our ongoing assistance and sacrifice. When our self-worth is affected by the extent to which we can look after or fix the other person, this is an important warning sign that our helping role may have crossed the line from being helpful to being potentially detrimental. Anger, guilt, resentment and unhappiness can be an important signal that this dynamic has started to develop within your relationship.

ESTABLISHING HEALTHY BOUNDARIES

This brings us to the importance of boundaries in any helping relationship. Establishing healthy boundaries is about knowing what is OK for you and what is not OK for you, in your helping role. In other words, it is being able to draw a line between a helping role that is driven by wanting to empower the other person, and a helping role that is driven primarily by a sense of duty, obligation or necessity to sacrifice your own needs for the benefit of others.

Anxiety is part of life, and part of being human. This means that any one of us can find ourselves facing a heightened level of anxiety, depending on what is going on in our lives. Sometimes, engaging with others who are experiencing anxiety can influence us, especially if we are feeling vulnerable or more anxious that usual ourselves. This does not necessarily mean that we cannot help others when we struggle with anxiety ourselves. However, it is important to have an awareness of our own mental state, and check in on that regularly when entering a helping role. If we recognize that the helping role is eclipsing our ability to care for ourselves, this may be an indication that some further boundary setting should be considered.

Establishing boundaries is also about being clear that, ultimately, the person you are supporting is responsible for themselves, and that you are responsible for yourself. Of course, we can help each other, strengthen each other, and step in for the other when things are difficult, but this is not the same as stepping in and taking responsibility away from the other person. Ultimately, each one of us is responsible only for ourselves (with the exception of when we are caring for a small child).

Of course, this does not mean simply leaving the other person to struggle, or walking away without concern. What it means is holding your own needs, and an awareness of the limits of what you can offer, alongside your willingness to help. A healthy dynamic means balancing your own individuality, life and identity, while consciously dedicating some of your time and attention to helping the person close to you who is struggling.

Again, let's look at what happened for Angela in her helping role:

Since learning about Catriona's difficulties with anxiety, Angela had blamed herself. She thought about all the times she and Robert may have somehow got it 'wrong' as parents, and wondered if perhaps they had made different decisions at different times, life would be easier for Catriona now. She worried that Catriona may not have been psychologically prepared for life at university, or that she may not have been equipped to cope with such a challenging academic course. Angela saw this as a failing on her part as a parent. The guilt that went with that made Angela feel that she had to do whatever possible to make it up to Catriona.

As Catriona's anxiety worsened, Angela gradually became more and more involved in trying to help her daughter. She phoned Catriona a number of times a day, and regularly drove a 100-mile round trip to deliver homemade food, to save Catriona having to worry about going shopping or preparing meals. Angela offered to phone Catriona's university tutors to explain that she could not submit her work on time, and suggested to Catriona that it may be a good idea to give up university and come back to live at home, where she would not have to worry about anything.

While this was going on, Angela withdrew more and more from her own life. Robert and their other two daughters felt disconnected from Angela, and grew increasingly concerned that she was not seeing her friends, doing things she usually enjoyed like golf and gardening, and she was becoming noticeably low and miserable.

BLAME, SHAME AND THE WIDER CONTEXT

The indirect effects of anxiety often impact many important relationships and contexts in the person's life. That might include family relationships, romantic relationships, friendships and wider communities.

In earlier chapters, we have seen how anxiety often leads to avoidance. Instinctively, fear makes us seek safety. One thing we all do in moments of threat is turn inward, in order to protect ourselves, and minimize our perceived threat of harm. In social terms, that can mean withdrawal from important relationships.

Changes in the relationship with the person close to you might be the thing you notice first as their supporter, because it impacts you, and may impact the wider family or social network. Depending on your relationship, you might notice changes in the person's mood, motivation, in their behaviour or in your intimate relationship.

When we notice someone close to us withdrawing, it is natural to seek an explanation. And it is natural for us to feel anxious ourselves, as we notice our connection with the person, or distance extending the space between us. When we realize that something is not quite right, we tend to seek an explanation, or to work out who or what is responsible for this change.

> "The strongest antidote to judgement is compassion."

One thing that can creep into the picture in this scenario is blame. When we notice an unwanted change in someone close to us, we can find ourselves seeking to place responsibility for that on someone or something. Of course, it is appropriate to expect someone to take responsibility for wrongdoing or causing harm. But in the context of helping someone with anxiety – or mental health in general – it is unhelpful to blame the person who is suffering for their own difficulties.

This can be particularly important in the context of families, social groups or wider communities. If we adopt a critical or judgemental stance toward the person who is suffering, it can isolate them further, and make the road back to connection and living well more difficult.

When I talk about blame, I am also referring to the blame and shame we almost inevitably direct at ourselves at some point in the journey of helping someone close to us who is struggling.

The strongest antidote to judgement is compassion. Ultimately you cannot control other people, but you may be able to influence them by keeping blame and shame out of the conversation.

When it comes to how we treat ourselves, checking the tone and attitude we use toward ourselves is key. It may come naturally to show others care and compassion, but we often find it difficult to extend the same attitude to ourselves.

Of course, there is place for self-correction when we make a mistake, or appropriately taking responsibility when the situation calls for it. But, just as it can be harmful to attribute blame to the person living with anxiety, it can also be harmful to unduly blame ourselves.

THE POWER OF REFLECTION

In any helping role, it is important to take time to reflect, and think about how you may be affected by what is going on in the relationship. This is especially important if you recognize that you may be prone to overlooking your own needs, or taking excess responsibility for the experience of the other person.

'Reflection' means thinking about what happened in a situation, paying particular attention to our own role, behaviour and influence. By doing this, we give ourselves a chance to recognize where and how we impacted a situation, but also where and how the situation impacted us.

Reflection allows us to acknowledge how something may be impacting us, and how that might be affecting our wellbeing, behaviour and broader relationships. It is a powerful antidote to being caught up in, and overly focused on, a helping role.

Some questions to support reflection:

- What happened?
- How am I feeling about what happened?
- How did my action (or inaction) influence the situation?
- How did the situation affect me?
- What can I learn from this?
- What do I need right now?

Sometimes, quiet personal reflection can be enough. Sometimes, using a journal can aid reflection, and help with processing whatever is going on. Talking things through with someone you trust, outside of the dynamic between you and the person you are supporting, is another space where reflection can take place.

There is an important difference between reflection and rumination. Reflection is about processing what happened, learning from it and acknowledging our own needs. That is a productive (though not always painless) activity that should bring us forward in our understanding of a situation and of ourselves.

"It is OK not to get it right every time, and it is OK to struggle."

By comparison, rumination tends to involve overthinking a situation, paying particular attention to what we perceive we did wrong, or what someone else did wrong, without moving forward or gaining any new insight. For reflection to work, there needs to be a focus on learning and meeting needs, rather than on repeatedly going over negative aspects of a past situation.

Remember, it is OK not to get it right every time, and it is OK to struggle. In any helping relationship, there will be times where you might feel helpless, clueless or as if you are making things worse instead of better.

Treat yourself with the same level of kindness and compassion you show the person close to you, or anyone else. You are doing your best.

Let's look at how Angela reflected on her helping role:

For Angela, self-blame for Catriona's difficulties drove her to take sole responsibility for Catriona's mental health. As this took hold, she found herself withdrawing from her own usual routine, commitments and passions, and focusing almost solely on Catriona's needs. Over time, Angela's extended family and friends noticed a change in her mood, and grew concerned that she was taking responsibility for Catriona's difficulties.

Alone, or in conversation with trusted friends, Angela was gradually able to reflect on what was going on for her. Through this process, she began to see that she was taking responsibility for Catriona and, in doing so, becoming caught in a dynamic that was not helpful to either of them.

Angela began to see that there was an important difference between supporting her daughter lovingly, and taking all power and responsibility away from Catriona.

For Angela, an important part of being able to step back involved letting go of the idea that she – or anyone – was to blame for Catriona's difficulties with anxiety. By practising compassion for herself, Angela was able to take back some of her time and energy. This involved practically scheduling in things that mattered for her own life, such as time with friends, her own work, exercise, gardening and making travel plans.

She was also able to hand responsibility back to Catriona, while continuing to support her with anxiety. There were times when this was difficult, but with support from her own family and friends, Angela was able to help Catriona without wiping out her own life and identity.

SUMMARY

- Check in with yourself regularly, and consider the impact on your own life when helping someone close to you with anxiety.
- Our emotional state can be a good indicator that we need to prioritize caring for ourselves. If you notice an increase in anger, guilt or generally feeling miserable, it might be a sign that something needs to change.
- Remember that you are not responsible for the person you are supporting. Consider the boundaries around your helping role.
- Spend time reflecting on what is working and what is not.
- Be gentle with yourself. You are doing your best.

FINAL THOUGHTS

There is a reason why this book is not called *How to FIX Someone with Anxiety*; nor is it called *How to SAVE Someone with Anxiety*.

By picking up this book, you have already done one of the most powerful things you can do to help someone close to you live better with anxiety. You have shown an inclination, an attitude and a willingness to respond to them in a helpful way.

There will be many factors influencing your loved one's anxiety over which you have little or no control. What you can control is how you meet them in their distress, and how you play your part as someone who wants to help.

When we have the privilege of being a helper in someone's life – whether it is for a moment, or for a long period – we form merely one link in the chain of experiences that might lead to change for that person.

In my work as a therapist, I am often reminded that the most important thing is not whether we ultimately get to witness someone emerge from a difficult time, meet their goals in their entirety and live well with difficult feelings. Sometimes we do get to see that, and that is great. But it is rare for one helping relationship to be the only thing that influences positive change for someone. What is more likely is that your influence will form one link in the chain of many influences, at different times and in different spaces.

So, don't be disheartened if the person's transition to living well with anxiety is not linear or smooth. Change rarely is.

Ultimately, we cannot control what extent someone will respond to our efforts to help. But we can do our best to create a good experience for the person who has trusted us to help them. And that might be enough to take them to the next stage of seeking help.

It might give them just enough confidence to try something new, which might lead to significant change. It might help them trust to the point that they are able to take more risks, and discover that they are more capable than they ever thought. It might do enough to let them realize that living well can mean living well *with* anxiety.

Good luck.

ACKNOWLEDGEMENTS

This book draws on knowledge and insight from the work of generations of psychologists, therapists, researchers and scholars. The work and dedication of former generations is what allows today's psychologists to help our clients in the way that we do.

Psychology and books have been in my life from the beginning, thanks to growing up in a household that prized both. It is not a coincidence that I am drawn to the classic psychology experiments of the 1960s, and to how these influence the way we learn and make sense of the world. My father, Finlay MacLeod, is my original teacher and mentor.

I am indebted to the trainers, supervisors, colleagues and many others who have influenced my development as a clinician. Your voices stay with me, making me who I am as a therapist and as a person. I owe a great deal to some outstanding supervisors, past and present.

The team at Welbeck Balance put their faith in me as a new writer. Beth Bishop has been patient, supportive and utterly kind on what has been a steep and rapid learning curve.

ACKNOWLEDGEMENTS

My husband, Andy Allan, makes my work possible. This book was commissioned during the lockdown of 2020. Childcare was off and libraries were shut. Andy pulled out all the stops to let me get on with it, against the odds. Your strength, consistency and compassion drive every word. Mairi and Finlay: you are our heartbeat.

Most of all, I thank every patient and client who has ever put their trust in me. Witnessing your journey is the privilege of my life. I hope I never stop learning from you.

ENDNOTES

i. Chambless, D.L and Gillis, M.M. (1993). Cognitive therapy of anxiety disorders. *Journal of Consulting and Clinical Psychology, 61(2)*, 248-260.

ii. Hofmann, S.G., Sawyer, A.T., Witt, A.A and Oh, D. (2010). The effect of mindfulness-based therapy on anxiety and depressions: A meta-analytic review. *Journal of Consulting and Clinical Psychology, 78(2)*, 169-183. And Forman, E.M., Herbert, J.D., Moitra, E., Yeoman, P.D. and Gellar, P.A. (2007). A randomized controlled effectiveness trial of acceptance and commitment therapy for anxiety and depression, *Behavior Modification*, 772-799.

iii. America Psychiatric Association (2013). *Diagnostic and Statistical Manual of Mental Disorders* (5th ed.). Arlington, VA.

iv. Covey, S. (1989). *The 7 Habits of Highly Effective People*. New York: Free Press.

v. Beck, A.T., Rush, A.J., Shaw, B.F., and Emery, G. (1979). *Cognitive Therapy of Depression*. New York: Guilford Press.

vi. Padesky, C.A. and Mooney, K.A. (1990). Presenting
     the cognitive model to clients. *International Cognitive
     Therapy Newsletter, 6,* 13-14. Retrieved from www.
     padesky.com. And Padesky, C.A., and Greenberger, D.
     (1995). *Clinician's Guide to Mind Over Mood.* New York:
     Guilford Press

vii. Padesky, C.A. and Mooney, K.A (1990). Presenting
     the cognitive model to clients. *International Cognitive
     Therapy Newsletter, 6,* 13-14. Retrieved from www.
     padesky.com.

viii. Burns, D.D. (1989). *The Feeling Good Handbook: The
     Groundbreaking Program With Powerful New Techniques
     and Step-by-Step Exercises to Overcome Depression,
     Conquer Anxiety and Enjoy Greater Intimacy.* London:
     Blackwell's.

ix. Chambless, D.L. and Gillis, M.M. (1993). Cognitive
     therapy of anxiety disorders. *Journal of Consulting and
     Clinical Psychology, 61(2),* 248-260.

x.   Polihronis, C., Cloutier, P., Kaur, J., Skinner, R. and
     Cappelli, M. (2020). What's the harm in asking? A
     systematic review and meta-analysis on the risks of
     asking about suicide-related behaviours and self-harm
     with quality appraisal, *Archives of Suicide Research,* DOI:
     10.1080/13811118.2020.1793857

USEFUL RESOURCES

BOOKS

Columbus, Kate and Samaritans, *How to Listen: Tools for Opening Up Conversations When it Matters Most*, Kyle Books (2021)

Kennerly, Helen, *Overcoming Anxiety, A Self-Help Guide Using Cognitive Behavioural Techniques* (2nd Edition), Robinson (2014)

O'Kane, Owen, *Ten to Zen: Ten Minutes a Day to a Calmer, Happier You*, Pan Macmillan (2018)

Tirch, Dennis, *The Compassionate Mind Approach to Overcoming Anxiety Using Compassion Focused Therapy*, Robinson (2012)

Wilson, Kelly G and Dufrene, Troy, *Things Might go Terribly, Horribly Wrong*, New Harbinger (2021)

GENERAL MENTAL HEALTH RESOURCES

UK

- o Mental Health Foundation UK: www.mentalhealth.org.uk
- o Mind UK: www.mind.org.uk
- o Rethink Mental Illness: www.rethink.org
- o Samaritans: www.samaritans.org, helpline: 116 123

- Scottish Association for Mental Health (SAMH) (Scotland): www.samh.org.uk
- Shout: www.giveusashout.org, text 85258
- Young Minds: www.youngminds.org.uk

Europe

- Mental Health Europe: www.mhe-sme.org
- Mental Health Ireland: www.mentalhealthireland.ie

USA

- HelpGuide: www.helpguide.org
- Mentalhealth.gov: www.mentalhealth.gov
- Mental Health America: www.mhanational.org
- National Alliance on Mental Illness (NAMI): www.nami.org
- National Institute of Mental Health: www.nimh.nih.gov
- Very Well Mind: www.verywellmind.com

Canada

- Canadian Mental Health Association: cmha.ca
- Crisis Service Canada: www.ementalhealth.ca

Australia and New Zealand

- Beyond Blue: www.beyondblue.org.au
- Head to Health: headtohealth.gov.au
- Health Direct: www.healthdirect.gov.au
- Mental Health Australia: mhaustralia.org

- o Mental Health Foundation of New Zealand: www.mentalhealth.org.nz
- o SANE Australia: www.sane.org

ANXIETY-SPECIFIC RESOURCES

In the following websites you can find guidance, support, advice and treatment options.

UK

- o Anxiety UK: www.anxietyuk.org.uk
- o No More Panic: www.nomorepanic.co.uk
- o No panic: www.nopanic.org.uk
- o Social Anxiety: www.social-anxiety.org.uk

USA

- o Anxiety and Depression Association of America: www.adaa.org

Canada

- o Anxiety Canada: www.anxietycanada.com

Australia and New Zealand

- o Anxiety New Zealand Trust: www.anxiety.org.nz
- o Black Dog Institute: www.blackdoginstitute.org.au

SUPPORT FOR SUICIDAL THOUGHTS

If you are finding it difficult to cope or know someone who is, and need to be heard without judgment or pressure, you can find information and support from the following:

Crisis Text Line (US, Canada, Ireland, UK): www.crisistextline.org

UK

- o Campaign Against Living Miserably (CALM): www.thecalmzone.net
- o PAPYRUS (dedicated to the prevention of young suicide): www.papyrus-uk.org
- o The Samaritans: www.samaritans.org

USA

- o American Foundation for Suicide Prevention: afsp.org
- o National Suicide Prevention Lifeline: suicidepreventionlifeline.org

Canada

- o Canada Suicide Prevention Crisis Service: www.crisisservicescanada.ca

Australia and New Zealand

- o Lifeline Australia: www.lifeline.org.au

ABOUT US

Welbeck Balance publishes books dedicated to changing lives.
Our mission is to deliver life-enhancing books to help improve
your wellbeing so that you can live your life with greater clarity
and meaning, wherever you are on life's journey. Our Trigger
books are specifically devoted to opening up conversations about
mental health and wellbeing.

Welbeck Balance and Trigger are part of the Welbeck Publishing
Group – a globally recognised independent publisher based
in London. Welbeck are renowned for our innovative ideas,
production values and developing long-lasting content. Our
books have been translated into over 30 languages in more than
60 countries around the world.

If you love books, then join the club and sign up to our newsletter
for exclusive offers, extracts, author interviews and more
information.

To find out more and sign up visit: **www.welbeckpublishing.com**

🐦 welbeckpublish
📷 welbeckpublish
📘 welbeckuk

Find out more about Trigger: **www.triggerhub.org**

🐦 Triggercalm
📷 Triggercalm
📘 Triggercalm

WELBECK
BALANCE

ENFANTS
DE LA PLANÈTE

Roch Carrier

Éditions Paulines

DU MÊME AUTEUR
DANS LA MÊME COLLECTION

Ne faites pas mal à l'avenir
La fleur et autres personnages

Composition et mise en page: *Les Éditions Paulines*

Illustration de la couverture: *Caroline Merola*

ISBN 2-89039-651-7

Dépôt légal — 2e trimestre 1989
Bibliothèque nationale du Québec
Bibliothèque nationale du Canada

© 1989 Les Éditions Paulines
        3965, boul. Henri-Bourassa Est
        Montréal, QC, H1H 1L1

La femme qui raconte l'histoire d'Ellesmere

Je voudrais te parler de deux femmes du peuple Inuit: une très vieille et une très jeune.

La très vieille s'appelait Oneekatualeeotae. C'était un surmon. Son vrai nom, personne ne le savait plus. Elle était la plus ancienne de toute la communauté. Peut-être avait-elle même oublié son propre nom? La très jeune femme s'appelait Ilrosiaq.

Oneekatualeeotae n'est pas un nom difficile à prononcer pour les Inuit. Il veut dire: «la-femme-qui-raconte-l'histoire». La vieille femme racontait toujours la même histoire. Les plus vieux, beaucoup moins vieux qu'elle, ne se souvenaient pas de l'avoir entendue raconter une autre histoire.

Que disait Oneekatualeeotae? L'histoire de son village. Elle n'y avait jamais ajouté d'anecdotes, ainsi que faisaient les autres raconteurs. Elle n'y avait jamais ajouté de blagues pour faire rire.

Elle était si vieille qu'elle n'avait plus intérêt à mentir. On se disait qu'elle devait dire la vérité. On l'écoutait avec respect.

Anciennement, disait-elle, quand elle était une enfant, elle habitait au Sud près d'une mer où le jour était clair pendant l'hiver. (Ici, elle s'arrêtait, le temps de penser à tout cela, et chacun observait son visage plissé et ses yeux fermés, presque aveugles, qui avaient vu tant de choses. Puis elle reprenait son récit.) Un jour, un bateau du Gouvernement était venu.

Un Blanc, qui représentait le Gouvernement, expliqua au chef du village que le gibier était plus abondant au Nord. Le Gouvernement avait décidé de transporter la communauté là où Dieu avait semé le gibier pour ses chers Inuit. Alors on ramassa tout ce qu'on avait: vêtements, fusils, traîneaux, chiens, viande séchée, fourrures; et l'on remplit le bateau.

Pendant plusieurs jours, le bateau remonta vers le Nord. Les vagues étaient hautes. Jamais personne n'avait vu dériver d'aussi hautes banquises: des montagnes blanches qui flottaient. Aucun des chasseurs n'était allé aussi haut vers le Nord. Enfin le bateau s'arrêta. Le Blanc du Gouvernement dit que le nom de cette île était Ellesmere. Le Gouvernement donnait à la communauté le droit de vivre, de pêcher et de chasser en cet endroit où il y avait plus de caribous, plus de phoques, plus de

poissons qu'au Sud. Le bateau repartit et il n'est jamais revenu. On était
au mois d'*arnalinnguutivik* (octobre).

Puis l'hiver a commencé. Dans l'île
d'Ellesmere, il n'y eut plus de jour. Les
plus sages, quand ils ont vu que la nuit
durait sans finir, ont pensé que le soleil
était éteint. Il fallait manger; les hommes sont sortis dans la nuit. Ils ont
appris à ne pas se laisser surprendre
par les ours blancs ni par les hordes
de loups; ils ont aussi appris à chasser
le gibier dans le noir. Le soleil ne revint
que six mois plus tard.

Oneekatualeeotae disait qu'Ellesmere n'était pas son pays. Son pays
était au Sud. Ses ancêtres dormaient
dans la terre du Sud. Personne n'y était
jamais retourné. Si elle n'avait pas toujours répété ce qu'elle savait, les Inuit
d'Ellesmere n'auraient pas su que leur
vrai pays était au Sud.

Quand elle se taisait, à la fin de son

histoire, les plus vieux baissaient la tête, fermaient les yeux et fumaient en pensant à leur pays du Sud. Les plus jeunes préparaient, pour leurs chansons, les guitares électriques.

Un jour, la vieille Oneekatualeeotae perdit la parole. Sa bouche produisait des sons qui n'étaient pas des mots. Puis sa bouche fut comme gelée par le silence. Depuis longtemps, elle ne pouvait plus marcher; on la transportait. Maintenant elle refusait la viande fumée. Elle refusait le thé. Elle ne caressait plus le front des enfants qui s'approchaient.

L'on sut bientôt, d'une cabane à l'autre, que l'heure était arrivée, pour «la-vieille-dame-qui-raconte-l'histoire», d'aller dormir avec les ancêtres.

Muette, aveugle, percluse, comment la vieille Oneekatualeeotae fit-elle comprendre à son gendre qu'elle réclamait d'être transportée au Sud, vers la mer de Baffin, dans ce village où elle avait été un enfant et où dormaient ses ancêtres? Pourtant il avait deviné son plus profond désir.

Le gendre d'Oneekatualeeotae était déjà un vieil homme. D'avoir trop souvent dérapé dans l'eau glacée, durant les chasses d'hiver, et d'avoir trop dormi dans des iglous en se moquant du froid, il était perclus de rhumatismes. Il demanda plutôt à son plus jeune fils, qui avait seize ans, de reconduire la vieille Oneekatualeeotae dans le village des ancêtres, à des centaines de kilomètres vers le Sud.

Ayarak avait des yeux vifs comme ceux d'un loup affamé. Les muscles, dans son corps trapu, étaient tendus comme ceux d'une bête qui va bondir. Il avait une cicatrice à la joue, souvenir ineffaçable d'une lutte contre un ours. Ayarak l'avait tué.

Il avait expérimenté de longs périples. Chaque hiver, Ayarak partait avec les hommes et ne revenait qu'au printemps, à la fin des chasses. Cette fois, pour se rendre à la mer de Baffin, au village de la vieille Oneekatualeeotae, le voyage allait durer une douzaine de jours. Du moins était-ce l'évaluation des vieux qui n'étaient jamais allés vers ces terres lointaines.

Ayarak chargea son traîneau: couvertures de fourrure, carabines, appareil radio, réchaud, bidons d'essence, viande de caribou fumée, boîtes de sardines, du *bannock* (ainsi appellent-ils leur bon pain plat), poisson gelé, viande de baleine, plusieurs carreaux de *murtuk* (ce sont des morceaux, découpés sous la peau de la baleine, qui se mangent comme bonbons) et des tripes de phoques. Ayarak attacha les traîneaux à son skidoo.

Dans le premier traîneau on coucha la vieille dame emmitouflée dans son

parka de phoque et dans une peau
d'ours polaire. Dans le second, on ras-
sembla tout ce qui lui serait nécessaire.
Ayarak mit son skidoo en marche.
Toute la communauté était rassemblée
dans un grand silence.

«La-vieille-dame-qui-raconte-l'histoire» croyait retourner dans son village; tous savaient qu'elle s'en allait au
pays de la mort.

— *Aukchunie!* (Au revoir!) cria
Ayarak.

Son skidoo fonça de toute sa puis-
sance. Ayarak et son convoi s'effa-
cèrent dans la distance enneigée.

— *Harrah*! (à la gauche!)

— *Aa-ah*! (à la droite!)

Ayarak parlait ainsi à son skidoo
comme il avait appris à commander,
tout jeune, à ses chiens.

Pendant plusieurs jours il descendit
ainsi vers le Sud. Les traîneaux étaient
lourds, derrière; il ne pouvait filer aussi

vite qu'il le voulait, la neige de la toundra était parfois comme une mer agitée, toute secouée de vagues. Ayarak devait éviter les crevasses dans la glace. Parfois de grands trous d'eau l'avaient perforée. Il conduisait son skidoo dans la nuit totale. Cette aventure était vraiment une affaire d'homme. Ayarak ne s'arrêtait que pour remplir le réservoir. Il savait reconnaître les caches d'essence que les Inuit disposent dans cet immense espace vide, pour les chasseurs. À son retour, il laisserait ici et là l'essence qu'il aurait en surplus.

Quand il s'effondrait de sommeil, très vite il construisait un iglou. Il déménageait à l'intérieur toutes les provisions afin que ni les loups ni les ours ne soient attirés. Il transportait ensuite la vieille dame; puis il bloquait l'étroite ouverture avec de la neige. Après avoir mangé, il dormait, épuisé.

Un matin, quand Ayarak tendit ses

mains pour aider Oneekatualeeotae, elle ne les lui saisit pas. À sa grande surprise, la vieille muette parla très clairement:

— Continue vers le village de mes ancêtres où je suis née; l'heure est venue pour moi de mourir. Je vais m'endormir. Ma vie s'arrête ici. *Nokomuk* (merci).

Ayarak connaissait la coutume ancienne. Quand les vieux doivent mourir, rien ne peut changer les faits. Il ramassa les objets dans l'iglou; il ne laissa ni essence ni nourriture. Il enveloppa la vieille dame dans ses fourrures. Il reboucha l'entrée de l'iglou et repartit en abandonnant Oneekatualeeotae comme elle l'avait demandé, comme c'était l'usage.

Beaucoup plus tard dans la journée, il pensa qu'il aurait pu retourner dans son île d'Ellesmere au lieu de se diriger vers le Sud. Après avoir abandonné la vieille à sa mort, pourquoi avait-il continué à descendre vers le village des ancêtres d'Oneekatualeeotae? Pourquoi ne s'arrêtait-il pas maintenant pour retourner chez lui? Chevauchant son skidoo, à une vitesse sauvage, quelle force l'attirait donc vers le Sud?

Il voyagea encore plusieurs jours. Il pensait à la vieille dame qui, au loin, dans l'iglou, dormait.

Ayarak atteignit enfin la mer de Baffin. Il trouva un premier village. Personne, pas même parmi les plus vieux, ne se souvenait d'un bateau du Gouvernement qui était venu prendre les habitants d'un village de la mer de Baffin pour les transporter au Nord, là où la nuit durait plusieurs mois.

Ayarak allait d'un village à l'autre; il questionnait. Personne ne se souvenait. Oneekatualeeotae avait-elle menti? Une femme qui raconte toute sa vie la même histoire peut-elle mentir? se demandait le jeune homme.

Beaucoup de choses tombent dans l'oubli, lui dit un vieux chasseur; personne ne peut savoir tout ce qui a été oublié dans le monde... Puisque tu sais l'histoire, toi, tu dois la raconter...

Ayarak, qui n'avait jamais aimé parler, raconta l'histoire de la vieille dame, son voyage en skidoo avec elle et son abandon dans l'iglou... Il racontait. On l'écouta avec respect, car il savait ce que ne savaient pas les autres.

Puis ce fut le temps de retourner au Nord, dans l'île Ellesmere, son pays. On lui fit une belle fête; on partagea la viande de caribou, on partagea la graisse de phoque, on but le sang délicieux. On lui demanda de raconter l'histoire de «la-vieille-dame-qui-raconte-l'histoire». Ayarak s'aperçut qu'il prononçait des phrases qu'il n'aurait jamais pu dire auparavant. L'âme

de la vieille Oneekatualeeotae parlait-
elle par sa bouche?

Après qu'il eut tout raconté, ce soir-
là, une jeune fille toute belle, la peau
blanche comme la neige où le soleil
brille, les yeux comme des charbons
dans la braise, se planta devant lui. Son
parka était tout décoré de fleurs bro-
dées; il n'avait jamais vu un aussi beau
parka.

— Je m'appelle Ilrosiaq, dit-elle.
J'ai quatorze ans. J'aimerais avoir un
enfant et partir très loin avec lui et mon
homme. Je n'ai pas peur, moi, de la
nuit qui dure plusieurs mois.

Ayarak savait se faire obéir des
chiens, il savait chasser les bêtes, mais
à une jeune fille, il ne savait que dire.
Dans sa bouche, les mots devenaient
une pâte épaisse. Son cœur battait si
fort. Tout à coup, il poussa un grand
cri, un hurlement qui fit sursauter, qui
se modula et se propagea.

— C'est le cri du loup dans la nuit, expliqua-t-il à Ilrosiaq.

— Je n'ai pas eu peur, dit Ilrosiaq.

Ils éclatèrent de rire.

Après un long voyage de treize jours, Ayarak rentra enfin dans son village d'Ellesmere. La longue nuit était terminée. Quand il présenta à sa famille la jolie Ilrosiaq, il y eut beaucoup de rires. On trouvait que la vieille Oneekatualeeotae avait beaucoup rajeuni. Quelques farceurs prétendirent qu'Ayarak connaissait un remède magique pour soigner la vieillesse. Chacun cependant voulut frotter son nez contre celui d'Ilrosiaq qui annonça:

— Ayarak m'a fait un enfant; vous le verrez.

La jeune femme raconta alors tout ce qu'elle avait vécu, elle le raconta souvent. Bientôt elle devint «la-femme-qui-raconte-l'histoire». Ce fut désormais son nom.

Histoire tendre
d'un petit lapin américain

Ce jour-là, en avril, au pied d'une montagne qu'on appelle Cheyenne, dans l'ouest des États-Unis, un lapin se tenait debout sur ses pattes arrière. Dans l'herbe nouvelle, c'était une boule grise tout arrosée de pluie. Le lapin ne broutait pas: il était trop petit. Il avait deux ou trois jours et des yeux pas encore ouverts. Un tout petit lapin égaré au pied d'une immense montagne; oui, bien petit, mais il ne le savait pas, il ne pouvait pas voir l'immense montagne de granite avec ses pics et, au sommet, la neige que le printemps n'avait pu fondre. C'était un lapereau bien seul, guère plus haut que l'herbe tondue.

Une très large route mène à la montagne où s'élèvent des barrières gardées par des hommes casqués et armés. Là, les voitures, les camions doivent s'arrêter. Des hommes en uniforme fouillent leur contenu. Ils inspectent les coffres, les caisses, les passagers. Des chiens dressés viennent flairer les véhicules; des hommes se glissent dessous pour vérifier si le châssis ne cache pas d'engin explosif. Après seulement, le véhicule a la permission de franchir la barrière.

La montagne est entourée d'une clôture barbelée. Lapinot était-il né là? Il était trop jeune pour le savoir, et même trop jeune pour avoir peur des chiens dressés que les hommes casqués retenaient avec autorité.

Un tunnel est percé dans le granite

du mont Cheyenne, un long tunnel où entraient des camions géants. Au bout, surveillée par d'autres hommes casqués et armés, une immense porte de plomb s'ouvrait. Pour t'en dire l'épaisseur, je devrais étendre les bras au maximum.

Lapinot se tenait debout, flancs nerveux; il était bien fragile comparé au plomb de la porte et au granite de la montagne. Mais il ne savait pas qu'il était fragile: il était trop petit pour cela. Il était trop jeune pour avoir appris qu'il y a de la faiblesse et de la force dans le monde.

Derrière la porte de plomb, d'autres tunnels sont creusés dans le granite. Ces tunnels mènent à une gigantesque caverne également creusée par les hommes. Entreprise surhumaine: des millions de tonnes de granite ont été extirpées du ventre de la montagne. Et pour obtenir cette tanière hallucinante, des milliers de travailleurs et de foreuses, des tonnes de dynamite, des centaines de pelles mécaniques et de camions ont uni leurs forces. Tout près, le lapereau ignore tout cela. Il ne sait même pas encore que l'herbe peut se brouter.

Dans cette caverne, «au centre de la terre», comme disent les vieux cowboys du Colorado, on a construit une ville où il n'y a ni fleurs ni parterre. Les maisons n'ont pas de fenêtres. Les murs sont d'acier, et les portes de plomb sont gardées par des hommes casqués et armés.

Les maisons ne reposent pas sur des fondations de pierre ou de béton mais sur des ressorts, de puissants ressorts en spirale. Si la terre tremblait ou était secouée par une explosion, la ville ne ressentirait rien.

Dehors, le vent s'était levé et jetait sur Lapinot l'haleine neigeuse des pics qui se dressent dans le ciel. Il frissonnait. Sa fourrure n'était encore qu'un léger duvet. Des milliers de personnes travaillent jour et nuit dans ces maisons sur ressorts. Ils sont jeunes ou vieux, hommes et femmes. Ils parlent au téléphone, écrivent sur des claviers.

La plupart, assis devant des écrans, étudient des cartes géographiques ou des diagrammes. Parfois un point apparaît, une étincelle sur l'écran vert; alors des centaines de boutons s'allument sur les consoles, des centaines de téléphones sonnent et, sur les claviers des ordinateurs, des doigts fébriles s'agitent pour demander une information qui aussitôt se lit à l'écran.

Dès qu'un nouvel objet est lancé dans l'atmosphère, on connaît tout de ce satellite, même s'il vole à des milliers de kilomètres de là.

Lapinot n'avait pas encore ouvert les yeux; il ne savait pas comment les humains vivent sur la terre. Il ne savait pas que, sous le mont Cheyenne, dans leur ville d'acier, des milliers de personnes surveillent tout engin lancé de la terre, de la mer ou du ciel qui pourrait menacer l'Amérique.

Lapinot ne savait pas où il était, il avait perdu sa mère. Il ne pouvait pas savoir que des hommes, sous la montagne de granite, ont le pouvoir de connaître ce que font d'autres hommes, en Russie, à des milliers de kilomètres. Il ne savait pas non plus qu'en cette Russie lointaine, il y avait peut-être aussi un petit lapin perdu au pied d'une montagne de granite sous laquelle on a bâti une ville pour que des hommes surveillent, devant leur écran, tout ce qui se passe en Amérique.

Lapinot ne pouvait pas savoir que les Russes connaissent l'existence de cette ville sous la montagne Cheyenne, en Amérique; il ne pouvait pas savoir non plus que les Russes sont au courant que là, sous 1 200 pieds (400 m) de granite,

les Américains les surveillent. L'igno-
rant lapereau ne se doutait pas que les
Russes souhaiteraient faire exploser
cette montagne. Il avait faim et il n'aimait pas cette douleur dans son ventre.
C'était sa seule pensée.

Sous le mont Cheyenne, entre les
murs d'une maison d'acier, dans un
petit bureau sombre, un homme, l'air
sévère, était assis. Sur sa table, il n'y
avait que des téléphones. L'un d'eux
sonnait. On l'informait que les Russes
venaient de lancer un satellite. L'étincelle, apparue sur l'écran, indiquait sa
trajectoire. Ce n'était pas une fusée
balistique. L'homme souriait. La paix
continuait. L'homme était un général,
responsable de tout ce qui se passait
sous la montagne.

Si l'étincelle à l'écran avait indiqué
la venue d'un engin explosif vers
l'Amérique, il devait en informer le
président qui aurait ordonné d'envoyer

des engins contre l'ennemi. Alors la planète aurait peut-être été anéantie et Lapinot ne l'aurait jamais su.

Le général, homme de grande responsabilité, était fatigué. Il paraissait beaucoup plus vieux que son âge, avec son front et ses joues creusés de rides. Heureusement, c'était l'heure de rentrer se reposer chez lui. Il suivit donc le tunnel vers la sortie. Les gardes armés et casqués lui ouvrirent les barrières et les portes. La lumière du jour l'éblouit. Qu'elle était belle, cette lumière, malgré le ciel gris et la pluie qui venait de cesser.

Que vit-il au milieu de la chaussée? Une balle de tennis? Non, cela semblait vivant. Le général releva ses lunettes sur son front pour mieux voir. Mais c'était un petit lapin! Il allait se faire écraser, l'idiot! Quelle tête folle! Parader au milieu de la route avec ces camions et ces voitures!

Le général descendit de sa voiture. Il recueillit la petite touffe qui frémissait et la glissa dans la poche de son uniforme. Puis il se remit en route. Dans le rétroviseur il apercevait, parmi ses décorations, la drôle de petite tête, les yeux fermés. Lapinot n'avait plus froid, mais il avait encore faim.

Un peu plus loin, le général s'arrêta à une animalerie. Il acheta une bouteille et une tétine. Il demanda ce qu'il faut donner à manger à un jeune lapin abandonné, trouvé au pied du mont Cheyenne.

Le temps passe vite quand on s'applique à faire avaler du lait sucré à un lapereau tout apeuré, qui ne peut savoir qu'on veut le sauver. Bientôt il fit nuit. La lune découpa sur le ciel le profil acéré du mont Cheyenne. La lune au-dessus, la pleine lune, faisait briller la neige au sommet. Et dans les mains

du général qui contemplait le ciel en
direction de la Russie, le petit lapin
frémissait encore, mais il était sauvé.

Perdu dans la forêt australienne

La plupart des gens ne sont pas allés en Australie. Pour eux et pour ceux qui iront un jour, voici une histoire avec un kangourou, un aborigène et un Australien.

Bill Greenway a 15 ans. Son père est architecte. Dans la famille, l'ancêtre Greenway était aussi un architecte. On peut voir à Sydney une petite église qu'il a construite, il y a près de deux siècles. La légende dit qu'étant un convict déporté d'Angleterre, il a, de sa cellule, dirigé les travaux de construction.

Le père de Bill a fait une crise cardiaque. Remis, il a vendu son entreprise pour se retirer à la campagne. La mère de Bill est la secrétaire du vice-recteur de l'Université.

Les fermes australiennes mesurent parfois plusieurs centaines de kilomètres carrés. Les Greenway ne possèdent que quelques kilomètres: une bande de terrain où bâtir leur maison et cultiver un minuscule potager! Tous les matins, Bill parcourt avec sa mère les 50 km de route poussiéreuse qui réunit leur hameau à la ville. Leur camion 4 x 4 est haut perché sur ses pneus antidérapants. À l'avant de la calandre est soudée une solide grille d'acier pour protéger le radiateur du choc des kangourous. Fréquemment, dans cette partie de l'Australie, des kangourous traversent la route d'un grand bond et se frappent contre les véhicules. Après la journée d'école, Bill attend sa mère pour retourner à la campagne. Il est souvent tard. Le soleil déjà peint de rouge le tronc des eucalyptus morts debout dans la plaine immense.

Auparavant, tout ce territoire était recouvert de forêts. Les colons ont brûlé la portion nécessaire. Puis ils ont divisé les champs et bâti routes et maisons. Là, dans cette lande sèche, vivent beaucoup de kangourous. On les voit en familles, bondir, s'arrêter pour regarder de leurs yeux vifs, flairer l'air et, tout à coup, disparaître car ils savent que vous êtes là.

Avant la venue des colons, un peuple noir et libre vivait à cet endroit. Il chassait le gibier, ne détruisant ni ne brûlant rien, car il adorait la nature qui lui donnait les biens nécessaires et la lumière qui lui faisait voir le monde. Il priait ses ancêtres dont il continuait la vie.

Bill Greenway a appris cela à l'école. Les aborigènes, comme on les appelle,

se réunissaient et, en silence, ils son-
geaient à leurs ancêtres disparus. Ils res-
taient ainsi des heures, parfois des jours
sans boire ni manger. Tout à coup,
l'âme de leurs ancêtres s'éveillait et
venait s'installer dans le corps de leurs
descendants. Ancêtres et descendants
réunis dans le même temps et dans le
même lieu, il n'y avait plus de mort,
mais la vie!

Le professeur a expliqué aussi que les
aborigènes d'aujourd'hui se réunissent
encore pour pratiquer ce rite que l'on
a nommé «dreaming». Bill Greenway
ne l'a pas cru vraiment. Il a vu souvent,
à la ville, des aborigènes flâner le long
de la rue commerciale comme s'ils
n'avaient pas à travailler. Il les voit en
petits groupes boire, l'air triste, une
bouteille d'alcool qu'ils se partagent.
Il sait qu'ils habitent des maisons négli-
gées dans un quartier modeste, qu'ils
regardent à la télévision les mêmes

émissions que tout le monde. Bill
Greenway a peine à croire qu'ils se
réunissent pour parler à leurs ancêtres.
Les aborigènes ont le téléphone dans
leurs maisons. Bill pense que les gens
qui conversent au téléphone n'ont pas
besoin de parler à leurs ancêtres.

Ce soir, Bill Greenway est revenu de
l'école plus tôt que d'habitude. Il rédige
son devoir avec pas mal de distractions.
Pourquoi est-il condamné à cet escla-
vage d'écrire le résumé d'un livre? Bill
aurait aimé être libre, sortir et aller, sur
sa moto, avec les amis, faire la chasse
aux serpents à l'étang. Mais il doit suer,
peiner. Sa mère lui dit: «Bill, le cœur
de ton père ne va pas bien, aujour-
d'hui. Reste avec moi, fais tes devoirs…
Je ne peux plus être seule.» Alors Bill
s'applique à faire de son mieux, mais
il ne peut rien écrire de bon. Pourtant
c'est un livre d'aventures.

Soudain, un kangourou saute dans

le potager. L'animal est jeune, roux. Il va faire un festin... et un ravage! Une catastrophe! Bill s'élance à la défense des carottes et des haricots. Quel courage! Quelle joie d'avoir un prétexte pour ne plus travailler. Bill sort sans faire plus de bruit qu'une ombre. Sans doute est-ce trop de bruit? Le kangourou s'arrête. Il écoute. Son fin museau en l'air, il sent le vent. Il frémit. Il se sent épié. Il est prêt à déguerpir. Bill, immobile, retient son souffle; il essaie de se faire invisible, de se fondre dans le vent, de n'avoir même plus son odeur humaine. Le kangourou tourne la tête. Bill voit ses petits yeux le regarder, et ses courtes pattes serrées contre sa poitrine. Bill veut protéger son potager, mais il ne veut pas que l'animal s'enfuie. Alors il serait obligé de rentrer se soumettre au supplice qu'a préparé pour lui son professeur. Que l'animal reste là où il est!

Le kangourou ne bouge plus d'un poil. Il écoute. Le chasseur et la bête s'observent. C'est un jeu. Le kangourou sait que Bill n'est pas armé. D'ailleurs Bill n'aurait pas la méchanceté de tirer, même un coup au-dessus de sa tête, pour lui faire peur. Il veut que le kangourou reste là le plus longtemps possible. Mieux vaut regarder un kangourou les yeux dans les yeux plutôt qu'un livre ennuyeux!

Le kangourou se penche et se relève. Entre ses petites pattes, il tient une gerbe de carottes dont il commence à grignoter les queues vertes. La bête ne craint pas le chasseur! C'est un jeune kangourou, sans expérience, téméraire. Pour qu'il se sente si sûr, sa mère ne doit pas être très loin.

Bill décide de tenter un grand coup. Il va le capturer. Il s'accroupit lentement. Il le surveille. Tout confiant, le kangourou grignote et s'arrache une

autre gerbe de carottes. Bill s'allonge
dans l'herbe. Il va ramper jusqu'au
potager, le contourner et surprendre
par derrière le jeune téméraire. Bill
entend les dents broyer les queues de
carottes. Il rampe vers ce trop confiant
voleur qui remplit son bedon de vita-
mines. Le kangourou ignore sa pré-
sence: il fait celui qui ne se sent pas
menacé. Bill va bondir sur lui, le saisir
par le cou, le soulever en évitant ses
coups de pattes. Il contourne le potager. Le kangourou, tout occupé à
mâchouiller, ne doit plus rien soupçonner. Bill, à quelques pas de lui, sent
l'odeur âcre de sa fourrure. La mère
ne s'est pas encore manifestée. Bill se
relève doucement pour bondir.

Le dos tourné, le kangourou ronge:
tel un gros lapin! Comme s'il voyait
chaque mouvement de Bill, pourtant
invisible et silencieux, il s'éloigne à
petits sauts, indifférent, méprisant pour

le chasseur, sans cesser de grignoter. Tout à coup, il change d'idée, se retourne, fait face à Bill, se dirige vers lui, s'arrête parmi les carottes, se fait une provision et, doucement, sautille vers les arbustes qui voilent l'entrée de la forêt de gommiers feuillus.

Bill ne va pas le laisser s'esquiver ainsi. Peut-être le kangourou n'a-t-il plus de mère? Il le suit encore. Il flâne: rien ne presse. Bill est patient. Il suit chaque mouvement d'un œil de chasseur averti. La bête ne doit pas le soupçonner. Il se dissimule parmi les branches désordonnées d'un palétuvier. Il veut rentrer à la maison avec ce kangourou dans les bras. C'est un animal qui doit se débattre avec force, mais à 15 ans Bill est grand et il a une force d'homme.

Les arbres sont vraiment hauts, plus hauts que lui. Le kangourou a disparu. Le bruit des feuilles lui a sans doute fait

peur. Il file. Des lianes créent un filet.
Le kangourou passe, mais le filet retient Bill qui essaie de le déchirer, mais
les lianes résistent. Les arbres sont très
hauts. Bill Greenway se serait-il trop
avancé? Non, il est encore tout près de
la maison. Il a seulement suivi le kangourou, un tout jeune qui ne faisait que
de tous petits sauts.

Que de moustiques! Ils entrent dans
les oreilles, le nez. Ces insectes l'étouf-
fent. Il ne voit pas ses pieds qui se
perdent sous les feuilles comme dans
une eau trouble. Bill n'a pourtant pas
marché longtemps. S'il se retourne, il
va apercevoir le hameau... Il s'arrête,
regarde d'un côté puis de l'autre; il
tourne sur lui-même et ne voit que
la brousse autour de lui, comme une
grosse tempête verte et sombre. Sa maison est de ce côté. Il s'élance. Ce n'est
que lianes, feuilles, troncs moussus:
un mur infranchissable. Sa maison est

donc de l'autre côté, mais la brousse est épaisse comme une nuit terrible.

Bill Greenway est perdu. Il n'y a pas d'autre bruit que celui de son cœur. La peur le suffoque. Tout à coup, un immense rire se moque de lui qui a si peur. C'est un koukaburra. Un oiseau peut-il être si méchant? Bill ne veut pas mourir. Il n'est pas loin de son hameau. Il appelle. On l'entendra. Il crie comme jamais on n'a crié en Australie. Jamais sur toute la terre un enfant n'a eu si peur.

Sa maison, son hameau, son père, sa mère, ses amis sont tout près, il le sait, mais la brousse efface ce qui existe. Il ne veut pas mourir. La brousse est cruelle pour les hommes blancs. Les journaux, la télévision rapportent souvent des morts... Bill a froid. Dans la brousse, le froid tue. Il ne sait plus si la nuit est déjà commencée au hameau. C'est un cauchemar, mais il ne dort pas. Le sol est mou sous ses pieds. S'il marche, il va s'égarer encore plus... ou peut-être va-t-il se retrouver? Le kangourou grignote tout près de lui. Il croit l'entendre. Des cris étranges déchirent le silence. Des glissements de bêtes rampent sous la végétation. Des ailes sifflent près de ses oreilles.

Bill Greenway appelle, appelle, il crie si fort qu'il croit que du sang coule dans sa gorge. Il pense à tout ce qu'il a fait depuis qu'il a aperçu son kangourou dans le potager. Il revoit la trajectoire de sa chasse. Il sait précisément où il se tient. Il sait où se trouve sa maison. Il va rentrer. Son père et sa mère ne se seront même pas aperçus de son absence. Il n'a plus peur maintenant. Il a cédé à un moment de panique. Pourquoi a-t-il eu si peur? Peut-être à 15 ans, n'est-il pas encore un adulte? Ce sont les enfants qui ont peur. À 15 ans, on est encore un peu enfant.

C'est pourquoi il a des larmes aux yeux.

Il sait maintenant comment rentrer chez lui. Il reprend sa marche. Le sol est gluant. La végétation est comme une eau trouble où nagent d'inquiétants insectes. Des lianes coupantes lui barrent le passage. Il ne peut pas avancer. Il est ficelé, il se débat. Il essaie de tout déchirer, mais il tombe. Il est épuisé. Il va dormir un peu.

Il doit s'arracher à la somnolence. Pour ne pas s'engourdir, il doit bouger, ne pas paniquer. Il doit secouer la torpeur caressante du froid. Il sait qu'il retrouvera bientôt son hameau. Là, juste derrière ces feuilles brille une lumière. C'est la lumière de la porte de sa maison! pense-t-il. Il se hâte. Que dira-t-il à son père?

C'est un feu tout faible qui fait un trou dans la forêt d'ombres. Bill hésite. Il craint de s'approcher. Impossible de

reculer. Il fait un pas, deux pas. Éclai-
rés par le feu, deux yeux pétillent. Bill
ne peut se cacher. On va bondir sur lui.
Quoi? Des dingos sauvages? Il hurle,
soulevé par la terreur de toutes les peurs
ancestrales.

«Pourquoi déranges-tu la paix des
ancêtres?», dit une grosse voix paisible.
«Approche-toi du feu. Il y a une couverture près du chien. Enveloppe-toi.
La nuit sera froide.»

Bill Greenway voit une vieille main
noire brasser des tisons et jeter au feu
quelques brindilles. La flamme pétille
et dévoile le visage tout maigre d'un
vieil aborigène noir, avec une barbe
blanche.

«Je suis égaré et j'ai peur», avoue
sans bravade Bill Greenway.

«Appelle tes ancêtres», dit le vieil
homme. «On n'a pas peur quand ses
ancêtres, autour, forment une grande
famille.»

«Je veux rentrer chez moi», dit Bill.

«La forêt était notre maison», dit le vieil aborigène, «mais l'homme blanc a attaqué notre maison... Notre peuple s'est trouvé sans toit et l'homme blanc se trouvera sans terre...»

«Je veux rentrer chez moi. Montrez-moi de quel côté est ma maison!»

Bill Greenway s'impatiente. Il ne veut pas écouter un vieux bavard. Il veut de l'aide.

«J'ai terriblement peur.»

Le vieil aborigène sourit lentement et soupire: «Les Blancs s'inquiètent, s'inquiètent, s'inquiètent toujours. Ils s'inquiètent quand ils s'égarent dans la brousse, ils s'inquiètent quand ils restent dans leur maison, ils s'inquiètent de la pluie, du soleil, de la nourriture... Les ancêtres ont connu la chaleur, le froid, la sécheresse, et ils ne s'inquiétaient pas.

Des milliers d'années plus tard, nous

sommes là, comme eux. Et nos descendants seront là dans des milliers d'années. Pourquoi tant d'inquiétude? Tu ne parles pas à tes ancêtres, jeune homme. Si tu les écoutais, ils te diraient de ne pas t'inquiéter, d'avoir confiance en la vie, d'avoir confiance en toi.»

Tout à coup, Bill Greenway n'a plus peur. Une grande paix le réchauffe. Les paroles du vieil aborigène ont guéri sa panique. Il s'enveloppe dans la couverture de laine et s'approche du feu. Le vieil aborigène a fermé les yeux pour retrouver le rêve de ses ancêtres.

Au-dessus de la forêt, s'approche le battement des hélices d'un hélicoptère. Bill Greenway est sauvé, il le sait. Des projecteurs fouillent la nuit. Au lieu de danser de joie, silencieusement, il s'assied devant le feu, à la façon du vieil aborigène.

La fleur du Brésil

Le Brésil est immensément riche. Pourtant, plus de 30 millions d'enfants y vivent dans les rues, sans famille, sans école, sans abri et sans avenir. Poussant comme la mauvaise herbe, ils sont les chardons des villes.

Je pense à Tancredo. Il a neuf ans, il fume des cigarettes. Il a une longue balafre à la joue à cause d'un coup de couteau; un grand l'a attaqué pour lui voler ses fruits. Tancredo vit dans les rues; le soir, sa maison est le seuil d'une porte cochère bordant le trottoir. Tous les soirs, il revient avec une fleur. Il aime les fleurs. Il réussit toujours à en

voler à quelque commerçante. Alors il
revient avec sa fleur, déplie un journal
sur le seuil de la porte, et s'étend pour
dormir. Sur le trottoir, dans la rue, la
vie tumultueuse de Sâo Paulo continue.
Musique, cris, lumières, bruits, caout-
chouc brûlé: cela coule, agité, fou,
puissant. Tancredo est déjà endormi.

Il a mangé aujourd'hui, mais il res-
sent une brûlure à l'abdomen comme
ces jours où il ne mange pas. Il a été
chanceux: il a réussi à arracher son
sac à une grosse dame qui hurlait en
anglais. Dans le sac, il y avait des
bijoux, des cartes de crédit et un tas de
dollars. Le chef de Tancredo a pris sa
part, ses amis ont partagé avec lui; avec
le reste de la fortune, il est allé s'asseoir
à un restaurant. On l'a jeté dehors
comme un chat plein de puces. Heureusement, il avait eu le temps de fourrer
dans ses poches les ustensiles. Insulté
parce qu'il avait été rejeté de cette

manière, Tancredo a commencé à
invectiver les gens qui mangeaient et
buvaient. Un touriste s'est levé. Tancredo l'a regardé avec son air de tigre
prêt à griffer. C'était tout simplement
un touriste comme les autres, bête,
attendri, qui lui offrait un beau dollar.
«Un dollar, même américain, ce n'est
pas beaucoup», a dit Tancredo. Dans
la rue, il a appris un peu de toutes les
langues. Le touriste, riant de la remar-
que de Tancredo, lui a donné d'autres
dollars. Tancredo est reparti en étant
très poli. Le touriste a repris sa place
en disant qu'il était bien triste que de
si gentils garçons soient forcés de men-
dier dans un pays aussi beau et riche
que le Brésil. Tancredo lui avait subti-
lisé sa caméra.

Il a réussi à manger un vrai repas
après l'avoir payé à l'avance et payé
très cher. Il posait un à un les dollars
sur le comptoir, mais le patron en récla-

mait toujours d'autres en tenant l'as-
siette devant le nez de Tancredo. Il
payait. Il était riche aujourd'hui et il
payait comme les riches. Le reste de sa
fortune, il se l'est fait arracher par les
pivetes de la rue.

Ce fut une vraie bonne journée! Il
n'a pas souvent autant de chance. Certains jours, tout va mal. Les touristes
ne se laissent pas dépouiller, les ven-
deurs de fruits le surveillent et le chas-
sent; il se fait battre par les plus grands
parce qu'il revient bredouille, sans une
montre, sans un portefeuille, sans rien.

Parfois, Tancredo se rappelle les
premiers jours à Sâo Paulo. Jamais
il n'avait vu une aussi grande ville.
Jamais il n'avait vu des millions de
gens. Jamais il n'avait vu de si beaux
buildings. Ils sont si hauts qu'on se
demande comment cela peut tenir
debout. Ces buildings sont pleins de
gens riches, pense-t-il. Auparavant,

Tancredo habitait au nord du Brésil. La sécheresse s'éternisait, on n'y avait plus rien à manger. Alors la famille de Tancredo a décidé de descendre vers le sud, où il n'y avait pas de sécheresse. Elle comptait 22 enfants, de tous âges. Ils ont dormi dans les champs, entassés les uns sur les autres lorsqu'il faisait froid la nuit; ils ont dormi dans les rues des villes. Ne trouvant jamais de travail, ils ont appris à voler des légumes, des fruits, des animaux parfois. Ils se sont même aventurés à briser des fenêtres de voitures. Les plus grands revenaient souvent avec des sacs à main ou des portefeuilles. Toute la famille est parvenue à Sao Paulo, la ville la plus riche du Brésil, croyait-on. Ils se sont dirigés vers une *favela*. Là habitent les pauvres du Brésil. C'est un bidonville: des cabanes bâties de morceaux de tôle, de bois, de carton amassés dans les dépotoirs ou le long des rues. Aucune cabane ne pouvait loger 22 enfants. Alors le père de Tancredo prit une décision. La famille devait se séparer. Chacun devait se débrouiller pour lui-même.

Au soir de la première journée, sans avoir mangé, le petit Tancredo s'est endormi en errant. Il était tombé sur le trottoir sans se réveiller. Quelqu'un l'a roulé du pied vers le seuil d'une porte cochère. Depuis, Tancredo est toujours revenu dormir à cet endroit. C'est sa place. Il paye son loyer. Tous les soirs, de grands *pivetes* viennent percevoir la somme due. Tancredo aime Sâo Paulo. La vie y est belle.

Aujourd'hui il a eu toute la chance du monde. Il a mangé et il goûte un grand bonheur. Sa tête est pleine de nuages. Il les voit, colorés, danser doucement. C'est un bien agréable vertige. Tancredo est heureux. Il se sent bien, chez lui, sur le seuil de la porte cochère.

Il va dormir une bonne nuit. La vie
continue dans la rue. La foule, pressée,
agitée, criarde, défile tout près de lui.
Les talons aigus des dames et les talons
pesants des hommes pourraient écraser sa main ou son pied. Tancredo est
complètement heureux. Il a reniflé de
la colle. Tancredo devient toujours
heureux quand il renifle de la colle: il
n'a plus faim, il n'a plus peur, il n'a
plus froid, il ne s'ennuie plus de sa
famille, il ne se sent plus seul. Sur le
seuil de la porte cochère, Tancredo
est heureux comme un roi, heureux
comme ces anciens rois du Brésil. Ce
soir il est le roi du Brésil. Il murmure
pour lui-même les mots d'une chanson
bien connue.

Quand les grands l'ont vu arriver
avec la caméra dérobée au touriste
généreux, ils lui ont dit:

«Aujourd'hui, on a la meilleure colle
qu'on n'a jamais eue. Forte comme de

la dynamite. Avec ça, on monte plus
vite qu'en fusée! C'est de la colle pour
hommes... Toi, Tancredo, t'as pas
encore un seul poil sur le corps... La
colle est pas pour toi... excepté si tu
paies le prix. On te donne la colle et tu
donnes ta caméra.»

Il a donné sa caméra et il a eu la permission de renifler la colle avec les
grands. Il était fier. Il doit toujours
payer parce qu'il est petit. Un jour, il
sera grand et les petits devront payer...
Il deviendra très grand, Tancredo, et
les petits paieront très cher.

La colle n'était pas plus forte que les
autres jours. C'était la même. Pourquoi les grands lui ont-ils dit que c'était
une colle spéciale? Pourquoi la lui ont-
ils fait payer avec sa caméra? C'était
peut-être une colle vraiment spéciale.
Tancredo n'osa rien dire, rien demander. Les grands se seraient moqués de
lui s'il ne savait pas distinguer une colle

ordinaire d'une colle très forte. Et l'odeur venait frapper dans sa tête comme des coups de marteau. Ah! elle était forte cette colle...

Il est si heureux maintenant. Il est couché sur le seuil de sa porte cochère, mais en même temps il vole, dans ce beau ciel du Brésil, qui n'est pas encore noir et qui a un goût d'eau fraîche. Tancredo est si heureux. Des adultes, qui travaillent certainement pour la police, viennent rencontrer les enfants des rues et leur disent que renifler de la colle peut causer des fissures au cerveau. Les adultes prédisent toujours la fin du monde... Des fissures au cerveau... Qu'est-ce que cela veut dire? se demande Tancredo. Si cela fait mal, alors, le temps sera venu de renifler encore de la colle! Il redeviendra heureux comme ce soir. Il était si malheureux quand la famille habitait le «Nordeste». La vie est belle maintenant...

Quelque chose crie tout près de Tancredo. Crie encore. La grosse voix in-
siste. Il pense tout à coup que c'est
une grosse bête sauvage. Tancredo est
effrayé, mais il ne peut bouger. Son
corps est trop mou. Sa tête tourne.
Finalement, il ne réussit qu'à avoir des
larmes aux yeux. Il a eu peur pour rien.
Ce n'est que le chauffeur. Il saisit Tancredo par la taille et l'enlève du seuil
de la porte cochère. Ensuite le chauffeur ouvre les deux battants de la porte.
Derrière, de l'autre côté du mur, Tancredo sait l'existence d'un grand jardin
vert tout décoré de dessins en fleurs. Il
ne regarde plus maintenant. Il sait qu'il
y a aussi une maison faite comme un
château. Le chauffeur retourne à sa
voiture. Tancredo sait que c'est une
Mercedes, un château noir et luisant
sur roues. Il la regarde entrer. Sur la
banquette arrière, Tancredo aperçoit
Madame et Monsieur. Ils sont allés à

une fête. Tancredo le devine à leur habillement. Le chauffeur referme les deux battants de la porte cochère. Tancredo est tout étourdi. Il retourne à son seuil. Le journal sur lequel il dormait n'a pas été déplacé par le passage de la Mercedes. Tancredo va dormir encore, il a tant sommeil. La voiture a écrasé sa fleur.

Tancredo ne peut pas dormir sans une fleur. Ivre, la tête endolorie, les yeux perdus, les jambes molles, il part, à travers la foule, à la recherche d'une commerçante à qui il pourrait voler une fleur pour la nuit.

Éphraïm ne voulait plus vivre en Israël

Israël: c'est une grande histoire et un tout petit pays. Pour le défendre, les Israéliens se sont montrés, peut-être, les meilleurs soldats du monde. À dix-huit ans, les filles comme les garçons deviennent soldats. Le pays a besoin de tous. L'ennemi peut frapper à tout moment. Les soldats d'Israël ne dorment pas. L'ennemi sait qu'Israël ne dort pas. Tous les jours, l'ennemi essaie de porter un coup. Souvent de jeunes soldats sont frappés. Il faut veiller.

Mitraillette à l'épaule, les amoureux marchent main dans la main. Les soldats montent dans l'autobus avec leur arme. Ils font du stop le long des routes, tenant leur mitraillette. Presque toujours, ils sont très jeunes. Ils sont très beaux, ces garçons et ces filles. Ils sont joyeux. Les casernes d'Israël débordent de rires. Cependant, l'ennemi est tout près. Il ne faut pas lui donner le temps d'attaquer. Alors, même lorsqu'ils rient, chantent, discutent, les soldats d'Israël n'oublient pas l'ennemi.

Israël est tout jeune, mais il a connu tant de guerres. La paix n'y est qu'un rêve. Certains jours, le rêve semble impossible. Tout désir de paix se transforme en devoir de faire la guerre. Les Israéliens ont fait miraculeusement pousser dans le désert les meilleurs fruits du monde, mais la paix semble ne pas pouvoir prendre racine en cette terre aride.

Parmi ceux qui rêvent de paix, per-

sonne ne la souhaite autant que les adolescents. Dans trois ans, deux ans, un
an, ils devront endosser l'uniforme
militaire. Ils savent que plusieurs ne
reviendront pas. Dans leur famille, un
frère, une sœur, un cousin a perdu la
vie au service militaire. Chaque famille
d'Israël a sacrifié l'un de ses membres.
Ils savent que, dans certains pays
d'Amérique ou d'Europe, la paix règne
et les jeunes peuvent vivre, poursuivre
leurs études et devenir adultes... Alors
les jeunes Israéliens rêvent comme il
doit être beau d'étudier, d'écouter de
la musique, de danser, de jouer sans
penser à un ennemi tout près qui se
prépare à vous surprendre. La paix ne
semble pas vouloir s'approcher d'Israël
où il faut se protéger, s'armer, cons-
truire des murs, installer des clôtures
barbelées et des systèmes d'alarme. Les
jeunes Israéliens ne peuvent pas être
tout simplement insouciants comme les

jeunes d'Amérique. Est-ce que je parle
trop? Je crois bien que je devais te
dire tout cela avant de te présenter
Éphraïm...

Il avait quinze ans. Il était né en
Israël. Ses grands-parents avaient sur-
vécu aux massacres de la guerre en
Roumanie et ils étaient venus se ré-
fugier en Israël. Depuis toujours la
famille fait des affaires dans la fabri-
cation de chaussures. Les parents
d'Éphraïm continuaient la tradition.
La famille voulait qu'il devienne médecin.

Éphraïm aimait étudier; très tôt,
il avait eu une curiosité pour comprendre la vie. Il avait décortiqué des fleurs,
il avait éventré des sauterelles, des gre-
nouilles, il avait disséqué des souris, il
avait collectionné des serpents; sa
chambre avait l'odeur d'une morgue.
Des morceaux de plantes ou d'animaux
pourrissaient dans toutes sortes de so-

lutions de toutes sortes de couleurs.
Éphraïm ne voyait rien sans l'exami-
ner ensuite au microscope. Après l'école, il arrêtait à la pharmacie de son
oncle Shabtai Lifschitz et il questionnait l'homme des médicaments.

Éphraïm était l'un des meilleurs
joueurs de soccer de l'école. Sa famille
était heureuse. Il excellait dans le sport
comme dans l'apprentissage des con-
naissances. En plus de l'hébreu et de
l'anglais, il apprenait l'allemand et l'es-
pagnol. Sa famille insistait sur cette
étude, disant que plus une personne
maîtrise de langues, plus libre elle est.
Éphraïm aimait la musique; au piano,
il avait autant de plaisir à jouer Bach
que Duke Ellington. Quelqu'un qui sait
jouer de la musique peut toujours
gagner sa nourriture, lui avait enseigné
sa famille. Éphraïm serait le premier
médecin de la famille. Ce serait pour
tous une bénédiction de Yahvé.

À travers les guerres, les déchire-
ments politiques, la famille était restée
attachée aux traditions et aux princi-
pes qui avaient assuré la survie des Juifs
à travers leur histoire d'errance. Elle
était fière de chacun de ses membres.
Aucun n'avait trahi. Plusieurs de ses
enfants se préparaient, à l'école, à la
vie adulte mais les plus grands espoirs
reposaient sur Éphraïm. Il deviendrait
médecin. Avec son intelligence discipli-
née et curieuse, il deviendrait un grand
médecin. Il avait toujours été intéressé
à chercher pourquoi et comment vivent
les êtres. Il continuerait sans doute
à chercher. N'avait-il pas toujours
dormi dans un laboratoire? Sa chambre débordait de pots, d'échantillons de
tubes, de cornues, d'ossements, d'insectes, de peaux séchées. La famille
allait donner au pays, peut-être, un
grand savant. En fabriquant des chaussures luxueuses, elle avait toujours servi

la richesse; grâce à Éphraïm, elle serait aussi au service de la douleur des hommes. Yahvé avait choisi Éphraïm et le guiderait, le protégerait pendant les années du service militaire: ensuite il entrerait à l'Université Hébraïque de Jérusalem.

Éphraïm ne savait plus s'il voulait encore devenir médecin. Il était devenu impatient de quitter l'école où, disait-il, il n'apprenait rien. Auparavant, chaque jour ouvrait un nouvel horizon; tous les soirs il se mettait au lit en sachant quelque chose qu'il ignorait à son lever. Maintenant, lorsqu'il s'allongeait sous ses couvertures, il n'était que fatigué. Il se sentait, à l'école, comme dans un incubateur tiède où l'on faisait mûrir les élèves en attendant qu'ils soient prêts pour le service militaire.

Autrefois, la nuit lui semblait trop longue et dormir lui était une perte de temps. Souvent, pour tromper l'inter-

diction de ses parents, il lisait avec une
lampe de poche sous ses couvertures.
Il lui arrivait aussi de se lever pour faire
sur son ordinateur quelques calculs
qu'il ne pouvait développer dans sa
tête. Maintenant, la nuit lui paraissait
trop courte. Il se levait avec peine et
sommeillait en salle de classe. Il ne lisait
plus sous les couvertures ni même à la
clarté du jour. Après une partie pourtant gagnée, il annonça à l'instructeur
qu'il ne pouvait plus jouer au soccer à
cause d'une douleur dans son dos. Le
médecin examina la colonne vertébrale
d'Éphraïm aux rayons X. Il ne décou-
vrit rien. Il diagnostiqua une fatigue,
un surmenage propre aux adolescents
qui grandissent et il écrivit une note
pour prescrire un congé de sports à
Éphraïm.

Ce dernier prit non seulement congé
de soccer, mais il fut quelques jours
sans se présenter à l'école. Quand la

famille l'apprit, il dut s'expliquer. Il raconta qu'il avait passé ce temps près de la mer, à marcher, car il avait des nausées et des migraines. S'il n'en avait pas parlé, c'était pour éviter des soucis à sa famille. On le comprit, on l'excusa, on lui fit prendre des médicaments: cet enfant grandi trop vite était trop sérieux et trop travailleur pour son âge. Il était épuisé, jugea-t-on.

Éphraïm n'avait jamais été un grand bavard: il était plus à l'aise avec ses livres, ses microscopes et son ordinateur qu'avec les jeux de la conversation. Les mots, maintenant, ne semblaient plus venir à ses lèvres. Il avait l'air de ne plus entendre lorsqu'on lui adressait la parole. À l'école comme dans l'autobus, il était seul.

Agacés par son silence et sa distraction, ses compagnons l'abandonnaient. Éphraïm était satisfait: il ne pouvait plus supporter leurs farces répétées

ni leur insouciance papillonnante. Ne
savaient-ils pas que bientôt le service
militaire les tirerait de leur beau rêve
éveillé? Ne savaient-ils pas, que les
sergents du service militaire allaient
bientôt les mettre au pas? Et gauche!
droite! Et plonge la tête dans l'eau pour
apprendre à vivre! Et marche sur un
pont de corde qui se balance au-dessus
du vide! Et escalade un mur! Et rampe
dans la boue pendant qu'au-dessus de
ta tête sifflent les balles. Et puis, dans
ton uniforme neuf, va faire le guet près
de la clôture barbelée pour te faire
égorger! Et va à la frontière, en jeep,
pour te faire déchiqueter par une gre-
nade! Puis attaque! Va dans le pays
voisin terroriser des femmes et des enfants et fais-toi percer le corps de trois
balles par un adolescent qui a appris à
détester ceux qui te ressemblent! Voilà
ce que ses compagnons oubliaient.
Voilà ce qui le préoccupait.

Un soir de sabbat, la famille était rassemblée au complet, père, mère, frères et sœurs, grand mère et grand-père autour de la chandelle pour le repas de quatre services. Soudainement, d'une voix très forte, avec beaucoup d'assurance, et dans l'étonnement de tous, Éphraïm annonça:

« Je veux émigrer au Canada. Là, il n'y a pas de service militaire. Je ne veux pas devenir soldat. »

Le couteau glissa des mains de sa mère et tomba dans la sauce qui éclaboussa sa robe. Ses yeux se couvrirent de larmes. Elle comprenait enfin pourquoi son fils était si étrange ces derniers temps. Le grand-père était devenu pâle et sa barbe sembla plus grise. La grand-mère pensa: « Menachem va faire une crise cardiaque. » Le vieil homme plaida. Ses yeux brillaient d'une inquiétante lueur: la colère. Pourtant, il parla doucement, avec affection:

« La vie a toujours été difficile pour les Juifs. Quand ils n'avaient pas de pays, ils étaient persécutés. Les Nazis ont tenté de changer notre peuple en cendres, mais les mourants dans les fours ont prié très fort et Yahvé nous a entendus. Il nous a donné un pays, Israël. Il faut défendre Israël. Il faut nous défendre contre ceux qui veulent encore persécuter les Juifs. Éphraïm, tu vas devenir un homme. Israël a besoin de toi comme soldat... Tu dois te battre pour ton pays... pour tes parents... pour tes enfants... »

« C'est trop difficile ! » dit Éphraïm.

Ce soir-là, Éphraïm ne voulait plus vivre. Pendant la guerre, plusieurs membres de sa famille avaient péri dans les chambres à gaz des Nazis. Il décida de mourir comme les siens, par le gaz. Quand il serait seul, il se barricaderait dans la cuisine, il fermerait les fenêtres et il tournerait les manettes au gaz. Il ne valait pas la peine de vivre dans un pays où il faut sans cesse haïr quelqu'un et se battre.

Ses grands-parents, ce soir-là, l'embrassèrent avec une chaleur insistante. Éphraïm alla dans sa chambre et commença une lettre:

Épître à ma chère famille

Quand vous lirez ces mots, je ne serai plus avec vous. Je serai là où personne ne se déteste, là où personne ne se fait la guerre, là où personne n'est obligé de tuer parce qu'il aime sa famille ou son pays. Je vais périr comme tant des nôtres sont morts: par le gaz. Je veux, par ce choix du gaz, montrer que j'appartiens vraiment au peuple juif. Ne vous inquiétez pas pour mon âme, je vais mourir en récitant les poèmes que récitaient nos frères et sœurs dans les chambres à gaz des camps de concentration. Je ne veux pas faire mon service militaire. Je ne veux pas tuer quelqu'un. Je veux mourir parce que, dans ce pays, il est impossible d'aimer la vie. Chers parents, vous m'avez élevé pour que je devienne un médecin qui soulage les souffrances. Que voulez-vous faire de moi, maintenant? Vous voulez que j'apprenne à tuer. Je ne veux pas. Pourquoi est-il si difficile d'être juif?

Chers parents, vous avez souffert pendant la guerre, comme les enfants des Juifs. Pourquoi n'êtes-vous pas allés en Amérique au lieu de venir en Israël? Je n'aurai pas d'enfants qui souffriront d'être juifs. Je vais mourir et je serai un Juif qui n'aura pas fait de mal à personne. Loin dans l'histoire et loin sur la terre, les Juifs ont été persécutés. Je n'ai pas de honte à mourir comme tant des miens vaincus par des difficultés insurmontables.

Il était très tard dans la nuit. À ce point de sa lettre, Éphraïm tenta de réfléchir mais il s'assoupit, la tête posée sur son bras. Plusieurs heures après, il se réveilla. Étonné de s'être endormi pendant qu'il rédigeait la plus importante lettre de sa vie, il voulut continuer. Où était-il rendu dans ses pensées? Il relut sa dernière phrase. Que s'était-il passé? Quelque chose avait changé. Il avait fait une correction. L'esprit tout embrouillé par le sommeil, il relut. Cette écriture n'était pas la sienne. Il voyait plus clair. Il relut encore: « Je n'ai pas de honte à *vivre* comme tant de Juifs *triomphant* de difficultés insurmontables. » Éphraïm reconnut l'écriture de son grand-père Menachem.

Il quitta sa table de travail et rentra dans son lit, malheureux, honteux, coupable. S'enlever la vie par le gaz de la cuisinière... Il n'avait pas envie de

cela. Puis, il n'avait pas envie de mourir. Et Israël est un beau pays qu'il vaut
la peine de défendre. Israël est le seul
refuge au monde où les Juifs peuvent
trouver la paix; cette paix, il faut la
protéger. Si les Israéliens ont pu faire
pousser des pêches dans le sable du
désert, ils pourront peut-être faire
pousser la paix dans cette terre de
haine. Menachem, le grand-père, avait
raison.

«Je n'aurai pas de honte à vivre
comme tant de Juifs triomphant de difficultés insurmontables… Je n'ai pas de
honte à *vivre*», répéta Éphraïm.

Le vieil homme s'était levé durant la
nuit. La lumière filtrant sous la porte
d'Éphraïm l'avait intrigué. Il était
entré, pour trouver son petit-fils à sa
table, la tête posée sur une lettre. Menachem put lire: «Lettre à ma chère
famille». Poussé davantage par sa longue expérience de l'inquiétude que par

curiosité, il lut la lettre. Troublé, il ne s'était pas aperçu qu'il n'avait pas ses lunettes. À la fin, il eut les larmes aux yeux. Cette peur de son petit-fils, il l'avait aussi connue. C'était plus de la terreur que de la peur. Malgré la peur, ou la terreur, le peuple élu devait toujours marcher, ne jamais se rendre. Maintenant que les Juifs étaient rentrés dans la terre promise, ils devaient bâtir le pays, ne pas démissionner sous la peur. Les enfants comme Éphraïm étaient l'avenir du pays. Ils devaient choisir la vie. Les larmes aux yeux, rêvant d'un jour futur où Israël pourrait offrir non la guerre mais la paix à ses enfants, le vieux Menachem avait cru que son devoir était de corriger la lettre d'Éphraïm. Il avait remplacé *mourir* par *vivre* et *vaincu* par *triomphant*. Ces mots résumaient sa vie et celle du peuple juif.

L'histoire de sa vie revint à la mé-

moire de Menachem: les fuites hale-
tantes dans les rues de Bucarest; les
longues semaines caché dans un grenier
froid et sans provisions, la fuite à la
campagne dans un camion à charbon,
la dénonciation et le voyage dans un
train à bestiaux vers une destination
inconnue; la vie dans un camp de concentration où les Juifs ressemblaient
plus à des squelettes qu'à des humains;
la musique du violon qu'il prenait pour
distraire les bourreaux; puis la fuite,
encore: à demi-mourant, il avait réussi
à fuir le camp de concentration. Plus
tard, il avait retrouvé sa femme, il était
venu en Israël et il avait planté des
arbres à fruits dans le désert. Non, il
n'avait jamais voulu mourir. Éphraïm
non plus ne voulait pas mourir. Il avait
quelque chose à donner à la vie.

Éphraïm se rendormit. À son réveil,
il avait un goût irrésistible de vivre.
Jamais la lumière ne lui avait paru si

belle. Il y avait tant de poussière accumulée sur ses tubes, ses éprouvettes, ses échantillons, ses livres. Il allait tout nettoyer. Éphraïm n'était pas de ceux qui disparaissent lorsque le peuple a besoin d'eux. À la table du petit déjeuner il fit claquer un baiser sur le front du vieux Menachem qui rougit. Chacun s'étonna de la soudaine affection d'Éphraïm.

Sommaire

La femme qui raconte l'histoire
    d'Ellesmere 5

Histoire tendre d'un petit lapin
    américain 19

Perdu dans la forêt australienne 29

La fleur du Brésil 45

Éphraïm ne voulait plus vivre en Israël ... 57

Collection

Lectures-ViP

Cette collection regroupe les plus beaux textes littéraires publiés dans la revue **Vidéo-Presse**. *Écrits par nos meilleurs écrivains québécois pour les jeunes, ces textes expliquent et décrivent l'imaginaire des adolescents, suscitent réflexions et initiatives, et évitent les prescriptions idylliques.*

1. PAS ENCORE SEIZE ANS...
   Paule Daveluy

2. ...ET LA VIE PAR DEVANT
   Paule Daveluy

3. NE FAITES PAS MAL À L'AVENIR
   Roch Carrier

4. LA FLEUR ET AUTRES PERSONNAGES
   Roch Carrier

5. LES SAMEDIS FANTASTIQUES
   Madeleine Gagnon

6. MAUVE ET AUTRES NOUVELLES
   Bertrand Bergeron— Marie-Andrée Clermont
   Pierrette Dubé — Cécile Gagnon — Mario Normandin

7. COEURS MALADROITS ET AUTRES NOUVELLES
   Ninon Larochelle — François Miville-Deschênes
   David Schinkel et Yves Beauchesne — Marc Sévigny
   Robert Soulières

8. ENFANTS DE LA PLANÈTE
   Roch Carrier

9. UN MONDE GROUILLANT
   Madeleine Gagnon

Imprimerie des Éditions Paulines
250, boul. Saint-François Nord
Sherbrooke, QC, J1E 2B9

Imprimé au Canada — Printed au Canada